T H E

History of a Literary Radical

& Other Papers

THE

HISTORY OF A

LITERARY RADICAL

& Other Papers by

Randolph Bourne

WITH AN INTRODUCTION

BY

VAN WYCK BROOKS

NEW YORK: S·A·RUSSELL

1956

LIBRARY OF CONGRESS CATALOG CARD NO. 56–9784

HARBOR SCHOLARS' CLASSICS EDITION

FIRST PRINTING MAY 1956

Designed by S. A. Russell

MANUFACTURED IN THE UNITED STATES OF AMERICA

ACKNOWLEDGMENTS

For their kind permission to reprint, the publishers wish to thank the editors of *The Yale Review*, *The Atlantic Monthly*, *The New Republic*, and *The Columbia University Quarterly* in whose columns many of these papers first appeared.

We are especially grateful to Mrs. Natalie Bourne Fenninger and Mrs. Ruth Branstater, sisters of Randolph Bourne, for their generous permission to include other papers, some of which had appeared in *The Dial*, *Seven Arts*, *Masses*, *Liberator and Century Magazine*.

For a volume of Bourne's papers now long out of print, Mr. Van Wyck Brooks wrote what we have always considered the most sensitive estimate of one writer by another. It is here reprinted as the introduction to this volume with two minor changes suggested by Mr. Brooks and the addition of a date of composition.

Contents

THE

History of a Literary Radical
& Other Papers

Introduction

RANDOLPH BOURNE was born in Bloomfield, New Jersey, May 30, 1886. He died in New York, December 2 1918. Between these two dates was packed one of the fullest, richest, and most significant lives of the younger generation. Its outward events can be summarized in a few words. Bourne went to the public schools in his native town, and then for some time earned his living as an assistant to a manufacturer of automatic piano music. In 1909 he entered Columbia, graduating in 1913 as holder of the Gilder Fellowship, which enabled him to spend a year of study and investigation in Europe. In 1911 he had begun contributing to *The Atlantic Monthly*, and his first book, "Youth and Life," a volume of essays, appeared in 1913. He was a member of the contributing staff of *The New Republic* during its first three years; later he was a contributing editor of *The Seven Arts* and *The Dial*. He had published, in addition to his first collection of essays and a large number of miscellaneous articles and book reviews, two other books, "Education and Living" and "The Gary Schools." At the time of his death he was engaged on a novel and a study of the political future.

It might be guessed from this that Bourne at thirty-two had not quite found himself. His interests were indeed almost universal: he had written on politics, economics, philosophy, education, literature. No other of our younger critics had cast so wide a net, and Bourne had hardly begun to draw the strings and count and sort his catch. He was a working journalist, a literary freelance with connections often of the most precarious kind, who contrived, by daily miracles of audacity and courage, to keep himself serenely afloat in a society where his convictions prevented him from following any of the ordinary avenues of preferment and recognition. It was a feat never to be sufficiently marvelled over; it would have been striking, in our twentieth century New York, even in the case of a man who was not physically handicapped as Bourne was. But such a life is inevitably scattering, and it was only after the war had literally driven him in upon himself that he set to work at the systematic harvesting of his thoughts and experiences. He had not quite found himself, perhaps, owing to the extraordinary range of interests for which he had to find a personal common denominator; yet no other young American critic, I think, had exhibited so clear a tendency, so coherent a body of desires. His personality was not only unique, it was also absolutely expressive. I have had the delightful experience of reading through at a sitting, so to say, the whole mass of his uncollected writings, articles, essays, book reviews, unprinted fragments, and a few letters, and I am astonished at the way in which, like a ball of camphor in a trunk, the pungent savor of the man spreads itself over every paragraph. Here was no anonymous reviewer, no mere brilliant satellite of the radical movement losing himself in his immediate reactions: one finds everywhere, interwoven in the fabric of his work, the silver thread of a personal philosophy, the singing line of an intense and beautiful desire.

What was that desire? It was for a new fellowship in the youth of America as the principle of a great and revolutionary departure in our life, a league of youth, one might call it, consciously framed with the purpose of creating, out of the blind chaos of American society, a fine, free, articulate cultural order. That, as it seems to me, was the dominant theme of all his effort, the positive theme to which he always returned from his thrilling forays into the fields of education and politics, philosophy and sociology. One finds it at the beginning of his career in such essays as "Our Cultural Humility," one finds it at the end in the "History of a Literary Radical." One finds it in that pacifism which he pursued with such an obstinate and lonely courage and which was the logical outcome of the checking and thwarting of those currents of thought and feeling in which he had invested the whole passion of his life. *Place aux jeunes* might have been his motto: he seemed indeed the flying wedge of the younger generation itself.

I shall never forget my first meeting with him, that odd little apparition with his vibrant eyes, his quick, birdlike steps and the long black student's cape he had brought back with him from Paris. It was in November, 1914, and we never imagined then that the war was going to be more than a slash, however deep, across the face of civilization, we never imagined it was going to plough on and on until it had uprooted and turned under the soil so many green shoots of hope and desire in the young world. Bourne had published that radiant book of essays on the Adventure of Life, the Two Generations, the Excitement of Friendship, with its happy and confident suggestion of the present as a sort of transparent veil hung up against the window of some dazzling future, he had had his wanderyear abroad, and had come home with that indescribable air of the scholar-gypsy, his sensibility fresh, clairvoyant, matutinal, a philosopher of the *gaya scienza*, his hammer poised over the rock of American philistinism, with never a doubt in his heart of the waters of youth imprisoned there. One divined him in a moment, the fine, mettlesome temper of his intellect, his curiosity, his acutely critical self-consciousness, his aesthetic flair, his delicate sense of personal relationships, his toughness of fiber, his masterly powers of assimilation, his grasp of reality, his burning convictions, his beautifully precise desires. Here was Emerson's "American scholar" at last, but radiating an infinitely warmer, profaner, more companionable influence than Emerson had ever dreamed of, an influence that savored rather of Whitman and William James. He was the new America incarnate, with that stamp of a sort of permanent youthfulness on his queer, twisted, appealing face. You felt that in him the new America had suddenly found itself and was all astir with the excitement of its first maturity.

4

His life had prepared him for the rôle, for the physical disability that had cut him off from the traditional currents and preoccupations of American life had given him a poignant insight into the predicament of all those others who, like him, could not adjust themselves to the industrial machine—the exploited, the sensitive, the despised, the aspiring, those, in short, to whom a new and very different America was no academic idea but a necessity so urgent that it had begun to be a reality. As detached as any young East Sider from the herd-unity of American life, the colonial tradition, the "genteel tradition," yet passionately concerned with America, passionately caring for America, he had discovered himself at Columbia, where so many strains of the newer immigrant population meet one another in the full flood and ferment of modern ideas. Shut in as he had been with himself and his books, what dreams had passed through his mind of the possibilities of life, of the range of adventures that are open to the spirit, of some great collective effort of humanity! Would there never be room for these things in America, was it not precisely the task of the young to make room for them? Bourne's grandfather and great-grandfather had been doughty preachers and reformers: he had inherited a certain religious momentum that thrust him now into the midst of the radical tide. Above all, he had found companions who helped him to clarify his ideas and grapple with his aims. Immigrants, many of them, of the second generation, candidates for the "melting-pot" that had simply failed to melt them, they trailed with them a dozen rich, diverse racial and cultural tendencies which America seemed unable either to assimilate or to suppress. Were they not, these newcomers of the eleventh hour, as clearly entitled as the first colonials had been to a place in the sun of the great experimental democracy upon which they were making such strange new demands? They wanted a freer emotional life, a more vivid intellectual life; oddly enough, it was they and not the hereditary Americans, the "people of action," who spoke of an "American culture" and demanded it. Bourne had found his natural allies. Intensely Anglo-Saxon himself, it was America he cared for, not the triumph of the Anglo-Saxon tradition which had apparently lost itself in the pursuit of a mechanical efficiency. It was a "trans-national" America of which he caught glimpses now, a battleground of all the cultures, a super-culture, that might perhaps, by some happy chance, determine the future of civilization itself.

It was with some such vision as this that he had gone abroad. If that super-culture was ever to come it could only be through some prodigious spiritual organization of the youth of America, some organization that would have to begin with small and highly self-conscious groups; these groups, moreover, would have to depend for a long time upon the experience of young Europe. The very ideas of spiritual leadership, the intellectual life, the social revolution were foreign to a modern America that had submitted to the common mould of business enterprise; even philosophers like Professor Dewey had had to assume a protective coloration, and when people spoke of art they had to justify it as an "asset." For Bourne, therefore, the European tour was something more than a preparation for his own life: he was like a bird in the nesting season, gathering twigs and straw for a nest that was not to be his but young America's, a nest for which old America would have to provide the bough! He was in search, in other words, of new ideas, new attitudes, new techniques, personal and social, for which he was going to demand recognition at home, and it is this that gives to his "Impressions of Europe 1913–1914"—his report to Columbia as holder of the Gilder Fellowship—an actuality that so perfectly survives the war. Where can one find anything better in the way of social insight than his pictures of radical France, of the ferment of the young Italian soul, of the London intellectuals—Sidney Webb, lecturing "with the patient air of a man expounding arithmetic to backward children," Shaw, "clean, straight, clear, and fine as an upland wind and summer sun," Chesterton, "gluttonous and thick, with something tricky and unsavory about him"; of the Scandinavian note,—"one got a sense in those countries of the most advanced civilization, yet without sophistication, a luminous modern intelligence that selected and controlled and did not allow itself to be overwhelmed by the chaos of twentieth century possibility"? We see things in that white light only when they have some deeply personal meaning for us, and Bourne's instinct had led him straight to his mark. Two complex impressions he had gained that were to dominate all his later work. One was the sense of what a national culture is, of its immense value

7

and significance as a source and fund of spiritual power even in a young world committed to a political and economic internationalism. The other was a keen realization of the almost apostolic rôle of the young student class in perpetuating, rejuvenating, vivifying and, if need be, creating this national consciousness. No young Hindu ever went back to India, no young Persian or Ukrainian or Balkan student ever went home from a European year with a more fervent sense of the chaos and spiritual stagnation and backwardness of his own people, of the happy responsibility laid upon himself and all those other young men and women who had been touched by the modern spirit.

It was an interesting moment. Never had we realized so keenly the spiritual inadequacy of American life: the great war of the cultures left us literally gasping in the vacuum of our own provincialism, colonialism, naïveté, and romantic self-complacency. We were in much the same position as that of the Scandinavian countries during the European wars of 1866–1870, if we are to accept Georg Brandes' description of it: "While the intellectual life languished, as a plant droops in a close, confined place, the people were self-satisfied. They rested on their laurels and fell into a doze. And while they dozed they had dreams. The cultivated, and especially the half-cultivated, public in Denmark and Norway dreamed that they were the salt of Europe. They dreamed that by their idealism they would regenerate the foreign nations. They dreamed that they were the free, mighty North, which would lead the cause of the peoples to victory—and they woke up un-

8

free, impotent, ignorant." It was through a great effort of social introspection that Scandinavia had roused itself from the stupor of this optimistic idealism, and at last a similar movement was on foot in America. *The New Republic* had started with the war, *The Masses* was still young, *The Seven Arts* and the new *Dial* were on the horizon. Bourne found himself instantly in touch with the purposes of all these papers, which spoke of a new class-consciousness, a sort of offensive and defensive alliance of the younger intelligentsia and the awakened elements of the labor groups. His audience was awaiting him, and no one could have been better prepared to take advantage of it.

It was not merely the exigencies of journalism that turned his mind at first so largely to the problems of primary education. In Professor Dewey's theories, in the Gary Schools, he saw, as he could see it nowhere else, the definite promise, the actual unfolding of the freer, more individualistic, and at the same time more communistic social life of which he dreamed. But even if he had not come to feel a certain inadequacy in Professor Dewey's point of view, I doubt if this field of interest could have held him long. Children fascinated him; how well he understood them we can see from his delightful "Ernest: or Parent for a Day." But Bourne's heart was too insistently involved in the situation of his own contemporaries, in the stress of their immediate problems, to allow him to linger in these long hopes. This young intelligentsia in whose ultimate unity he had had such faith—did he not

9

see it, moreover, as the war advanced, lapsing, falling apart again, reverting into the ancestral attitudes of the tribe? Granted the war, it was the business of these liberals to see that it was played, as he said, "with insistent care for democratic values at home, and unequivocal alliance with democratic elements abroad for a peace that should promise more than a mere union of benevolent imperialisms." Instead, the "allure of the martial" passed only to be succeeded by the "allure of the technical," and the "prudent, enlightened college man," cut in the familiar pattern, took the place of the value-creator, the pathfinder, the seeker of new horizons. Plainly, the younger generation had not begun to find its own soul, had hardly so much as registered its will for a new orientation of the American spirit.

Had it not occurred before, this general reversion to type? The whole first phase of the social movement had spent itself in a sort of ineffectual beating of the air, and Bourne saw that only through a far more heroic effort of criticism than had yet been attempted could the young intelligentsia disentangle itself, prevail against the mass-fatalism of the middle class, and rouse the workers out of their blindness and apathy. Fifteen years ago a new breath had blown over the American scene; people felt that the era of big business had reached its climacteric, that a new nation was about to be born out of the social settlements, out of the soil that had been harrowed and swept by the muck-rakers, out of the spirit of service that animated a whole new race of novelists, and a vast army of young men and young women, who felt fluttering in their souls the call to some great impersonal adventure, went forth to the slums and the factories and the universities with a powerful but very vague desire to realize themselves and to "do something" for the world. But one would have said that movement had been born middle-aged, so earnest, so anxious, so conscientious, so troubled, so maternal and paternal were the faces of those young men and women who marched forth with so puzzled an intrepidity; there was none of the tang and fire of youth in it, none of the fierce glitter of the intellect; there was no joyous burning of boats; there were no transfigurations, no ecstasies. There was only a warm simmer of eager, evangelical sentiment that somehow never reached the boiling-point and cooled rapidly off again, and that host of tentative and wistful seekers found themselves as cruelly astray as the little visionaries of the Children's Crusade. Was not the failure of that movement due almost wholly to its lack of critical equipment? In the first place, it was too naïve and too provincial, it was outside the main stream of modern activity and desire, it had none of the reserves of power that result from being in touch with contemporary developments in other countries. In the second place, it had no realistic sense of American life: it ignored the facts of the class struggle, it accepted enthusiastically illusions like that of the "melting-pot," it wasted its energy in attacking "bad" business without realizing that the spirit of business enterprise is itself the great enemy, it failed to see the need of a consciously organized intellectual class or to appreciate the necessary conjunction in our day of the intellectuals and the proletariat. Worst of all, it had no personal psychology. Those crusaders of the "social consciousness" were far from being conscious of themselves; they had never broken the umbilical cord of their hereditary class, they had not discovered their own individual lines of growth, they had no knowledge of their own powers, no technique for using them effectively. Embarked in activities that instantly revealed themselves as futile and fallacious, they also found their loyalties in perpetual conflict with one another. Inevitably their zeal waned and their energy ebbed away, and the tides of uniformity and commercialism swept the American scene once more.

No one had grasped all these elements of the social situation so firmly as Bourne. He saw that we needed, first, a psychological interpretation of these younger malcontents, secondly, a realistic study of our institutional life, and finally, a general opening of the American mind to the currents of contemporary desire and effort and experiment abroad. And along each of these lines he did the work of a pioneer.

Who, for example, had ever thought of exploring the soul of the younger generation as Bourne explored it? He had planned a long series of literary portraits of its types and personalities: half a dozen of them exist (along with several of quite a different character!—the keenest satires we have), enough to show us how sensitively he responded to those detached, groping, wistful, yet resolutely independent spirits whom he saw weaving the iridescent fabric of the future. He who had so early divined the truth of Maurice Barrès' saying, that we never conquer the intellectual suffrages of those who precede us in life, addressed himself exclusively to these young spirits: he went out to meet them, he probed their obscurities; one would have said that he was a sort of impresario gathering the personnel of some immense orchestra, seeking in each the principle of his own growth. He had studied his chosen minority with such instinctive care that everything he wrote came as a personal message to those, and those alone, who were capable of assimilating it; and that is why, as we look over his writings to-day, we find them a sort of corpus, a text full of secret ciphers, and packed with meaning between the lines, of all the most intimate questions and difficulties and turns of thought and feeling that make up the soul of young America. He revealed us to ourselves, he intensified and at the same time corroborated our desires; above all, he showed us what we had in common and what new increments of life might arise out of the friction of our differences. In these portraits he was already doing the work of the novelist he might well have become,—he left two or three chapters of a novel he had begun to write, in which "Karen" and "Sophronisba" and "The Professor" would probably have appeared, along with a whole battle-array of the older and younger generations; he was sketching out the rôle some novelist might play in the parturition of the new America. Everything for analysis, for self-discovery, for articulation, everything to put the

13

younger generation in possession of itself! Everything to weave the tissue of a common understanding, to help the growth and freedom of the spirit! There was something prophetic in Bourne's personality. In his presence one felt, in his writings one realizes, that the army of youth is already assembling for "the effort of reason and the adventure of beauty."

I shall say little of his work as a critic of institutions. It is enough to point out that if such realistic studies as his "Trans-National America" and his "Mirror of the Middle West" (a perfect example, by the way, of his theory of the book review as an independent enquiry with a central idea of its own), his papers on the settlements and on sociological fiction had appeared fifteen years ago, a vastly greater amount of effective energy might have survived the break-up of the first phase of the social movement. When he showed what mare's-nests the settlements and the "melting-pot" theory and the "spirit of service" are, and what snares for democracy lie in Meredith Nicholson's "folksiness," he closed the gate on half the blind alleys in which youth had gone astray; and he who had so delighted in Veblen's ruthless condensation of the mystical gases of American business implied in every line he wrote that there is a gulf fixed between the young intellectual and the unreformable "system." The young intellectual, henceforth, was an unclassed outsider, with a scent all the more keenly sharpened for new trails because the old trails were denied him, and for Bourne those new trails led straight, and by the shortest possible route, to a society the very reverse of ours, a society such as A.E. has described in the phrase, "democratic in economics, aristocratic in thought," to be attained through a coalition of the thinkers and the workers. The task of the thinkers, of the intelligentsia, in so far as they concerned themselves directly with economic problems, was, in Bourne's eyes, chiefly to *think*. It was a new doctrine for American radicals; it precisely denoted their advance over the evangelicism of fifteen years ago. "The young radical to-day," he wrote in one of his reviews, "is not asked to be a martyr, but he is asked to be a thinker, an intellectual leader. . . . The labor movement in this country needs a philosophy, a literature, a constructive socialist analysis and criticism of industrial relations. Labor will scarcely do this thinking for itself. Unless middle-class radicalism threshes out its categories and interpretations and undertakes this constructive thought it will not be done. . . . The only way by which middle-class radicalism can serve is by being fiercely and concentratedly intellectual."

Finally, through Bourne more than through any other of our younger writers one gained a sense of the stir of the great world, of the currents and cross-currents of the contemporary European spirit, behind and beneath the war, of the tendencies and experiences and common aims and bonds of the younger generation everywhere. He was an exception to what seems to be the general rule, that Americans who are able to pass outside their own national spirit at all are apt to fall headlong into the national spirit of some one other country: they become vehement partisans of Latin Europe, or of England, or of Germany and Scandinavia, or, more recently, of Russia. Bourne, with that singular union of detachment and affectionate penetration which he brought also to his personal relationships, had entered them all with an equal curiosity, an impartial delight. If he had absorbed the fine idealism of the English liberals, he understood also the more elemental, the more emotional, the more positive urge of revolutionary Russia. He was full of practical suggestions from the vast social and economic laboratory of modern Germany. He had caught something also from the intellectual excitement of young Italy; most of all, his imagination had been captivated, as we can see from such essays as "Mon Amie," by the candor and the self-consciousness and the genius for social introspection of radical France. And all these influences were perpetually at play in his mind and in his writings. He was the conductor of innumerable diverse inspirations, a sort of clearing-house of the best living ideas of the time; through him the young writer and the young thinker came into instant contact with whatever in the modern world he most needed. And here again Bourne revealed his central aim. He reviewed by choice, and with a special passion, what he called the "epics of youthful talent that grows great with quest and desire." It is easy to see, in his articles on such books as "Pelle the Conqueror" and Gorky's Autobiography and "The Ragged-Trousered Philanthropists," that what attracted him was the common struggle and aspiration of youth and poverty and the creative spirit everywhere, the sense of a new socialized world groping its way upward. It was this rich ground-note in all his work that made him, not the critic merely, but the leader.

It is impossible to say, of course, what he would have become if his life had been spared. The war had immensely stimulated his "political-mindedness": he was obsessed, during the last two years of his life, with a sense of the precariousness of free thought and free speech in this country; if they were cut off, he foresaw, the whole enterprise, both of the social revolution and of the new American culture, would perish of inanition; he felt himself at bay. Would he, with all the additional provocation of a hopelessly bungled peace settlement, have continued in the political field, as his unfinished study on "The State" might suggest? Or would that activity, while remaining vivid and consistent, have subsided into a second place behind his more purely cultural interests?

Personally, I like to think that he would have followed this second course. He speaks in the "History of a Literary Radical" of "living down the new orthodoxies of propaganda" as he and his friends had lived down the old orthodoxies of the classics, and I believe that, freed from the obsessions of the war, his criticism would have concentrated more and more on the problem of evoking and shaping an American literature as the nucleus of that rich, vital and independent national life he had been seeking in so many ways to promote. Who that knew his talents could have wished it otherwise? Already, except for the poets, the intellectual energy of the younger generation

17

has been drawn almost exclusively into political interests; and the new era, which has begun to draw so sharply the battle-line between radicals and reactionaries, is certain only to increase this tendency. If our literary criticism is always impelled sooner or later to become social criticism, it is certainly because the future of our literature and art depends upon the wholesale reconstruction of a social life all the elements of which are as if united in a sort of conspiracy against the growth and freedom of the spirit: we are in the position described by Ibsen in one of his letters: "I do not think it is of much use to plead the cause of art with arguments derived from its own nature, which with us is still so little understood, or rather so thoroughly misunderstood. . . . My opinion is that at the present time it is of no use to wield one's weapons *for* art; one must simply turn them *against* what is hostile to art." That is why Bourne, whose ultimate interest was always artistic, found himself a guerilla fighter along the whole battlefront of the social revolution. He was drawn into the political arena as a skilful specialist, called into war service, is drawn into the practice of a general surgery in which he may indeed accomplish much but at the price of the suspension of his own uniqueness. Others, at the expiration of what was for him a critical moment, the moment when all freedom seemed to be at stake, might have been trusted to do his political work for him; the whole radical tide is flowing behind him; his unique function, meanwhile, was not political but spiritual. It was the creation, the communication of what he called "the allure of fresh and true ideas, of free speculation, of artistic vigor, of cultural styles, of intelligence suffused by feeling and feeling given fiber and outline by intelligence." Was it not to have been hoped, therefore, that he would have revived, exemplified among these new revolutionary conditions, and on behalf of them, the lapsed rôle of the man of letters?

For if he held a hammer in one hand, he held in the other a divining-rod. He, if any one, in the days to come, would have conjured out of our dry soil the green shoots of a beautiful and a characteristic literature: he knew that soil so well, and why it was dry, and how it ought to be irrigated! We have had no chart of our cultural situation to compare with his "History of a Literary Radical," and certainly no one has combined with an analytical gift like his, and an adoration for the instinct of workmanship, so burning an eye for every stir of life and color on the drab American landscape. I think of a sentence in one of his reviews: "The appearance of dramatic imagination in any form in this country is something to make us all drop our work and run to see." That was the spirit which animated all his criticism: is it not the spirit that creates out of the void the thing it contemplates?

To have known Randolph Bourne is indeed to have surprised some of the finest secrets of the American future. But those who lived with him in friendship will remember him for reasons that are far more personal, and at the same time far more universal, than that: they will remember him as the wondrous companion, the lyrical intellect, the transparent idealist, most of all perhaps as the ingenuous and lonely child. It is said that every writer possesses in his vocabulary one talismanic word which he repeats again and again, half unconsciously, like a sort of signature, and which reveals the essential secret of his personality. In Bourne's case the word is "wistful"; and those who accused him of malice and bitterness, not realizing how instinctively we impute these qualities to the physically deformed who are so dauntless in spirit that they repel our pity, would do well to consider that secret signature, sown like some beautiful wild flower over the meadow of his writings, which no man can counterfeit, which is indeed the token of their inviolable sincerity. He was a wanderer, the child of some nation yet unborn, smitten with an inappeasable nostalgia for the Beloved Community on the far side of socialism, he carried with him the intoxicating air of that community, the mysterious aroma of all its works and ways. "High philosophic thought infused with sensuous love," he wrote once, "is not this the one incorrigible dream that clutches us?" It was the dream he had brought back from the bright future in which he lived, the dream he summoned us to realize. And it issues now like a gallant command out of the space left vacant by his passing.

VAN WYCK BROOKS.
September, 1919

The History
of a Literary Radical

FOR A MAN OF CULTURE, my friend Miro began his literary career in a singularly unpromising way. Potential statesmen in log-cabins might miraculously come in touch with all the great books of the world, but the days of Miro's young school life were passed in innocence of Homer or Dante or Shakespeare, or any of the other traditional mind-formers of the race. What Miro had for his nourishment, outside the Bible, which was a magical book that you must not drop on the floor, or his school-readers, which were like lightning flashes of unintelligible scenes, was the literature that his playmates lent him—exploits of British soldiers in Spain and the Crimea, the death-defying adventures of young filibusters in Cuba and Nicaragua. Miro gave them a languid perusing, and did not criticize their literary style. Huckleberry Finn and Tom Sawyer somehow eluded him until he had finished college, and no fresher tale of adventure drifted into his complacent home until the era of "Richard Carvel" and

"Janice Meredith" sharpened his wits and gave him a vague feeling that there was such a thing as literary art. The classics were stiffly enshrined behind glass doors that were very hard to open—at least Hawthorne and Irving and Thackeray were there, and Tennyson's and Scott's poems—but nobody ever discussed them or looked at them. Miro's busy elders were taken up with the weekly *Outlook* and *Independent* and *Christian Work*, and felt they were doing much for Miro when they provided him and his sister with *St. Nicholas* and *The Youth's Companion*. It was only that Miro saw the black books looking at him accusingly from the case, and a rudimentary conscience, slipping easily over from Calvinism to culture, forced him solemnly to grapple with "The Scarlet Letter" or "Marmion." All he remembers is that the writers of these books he browsed among used a great many words and made a great fuss over shadowy offenses and conflicts and passions that did not even stimulate his imagination with sufficient force to cause him to ask his elders what it was all about. Certainly the filibusters were easier.

At school Miro was early impressed with the vast dignity of the literary works and names he was compelled to learn. Shakespeare and Goethe and Dante lifted their plaster heads frowningly above the teacher's, as they perched on shelves about the room. Much was said of the greatness of literature. But the art of phonetics and the complications of grammar swamped Miro's early school years. It was not until he reached the High School that literature began really to assume that sacredness which he had heretofore felt only for Holy Scripture. His initiation into culture was made almost a religious mystery by the conscientious and harassed teacher. As the Deadwood Boys and Henty and David Harum slipped away from Miro's soul in the presence of Milton's "Comus" and Burke "On Conciliation," a cultural devoutness was engendered in him that never really died. At first it did not take Miro beyond the stage where your conscience is strong enough to make you uncomfortable, but not strong enough to make you do anything about it. Miro did not actually become an omnivorous reader of great books. But he was filled with a rich grief that the millions pursued cheap and vulgar fiction instead of the best that has been thought and said in the world. Miro indiscriminately bought cheap editions of the English classics and read them with a certain patient incomprehension.

As for the dead classics, they came to Miro from the hands of his teachers with a prestige even vaster than the books of his native tongue. No doubt ever entered his head that four years of Latin and three years of Greek, an hour a day, were the important preparation he needed for his future as an American citizen. No doubt ever hurt him that the world into which he would pass would be a world where, as his teacher said, Latin and Greek were a solace to the aged, a quickener of taste, a refreshment after manual labor, and a clue to the general knowledge of all human things. Miro would as soon have doubted the rising of the sun as have doubted the wisdom of these serious, puckered women who had the precious manipulation of his cultural upbringing in their charge. Miro was a bright, if a rather vague, little boy, and a fusion of brightness and docility gave him high marks in the school where we went together.

No one ever doubted that these marks expressed Miro's assimilation of the books we pored over. But he told me later that he had never really known what he was studying. Cæsar, Virgil, Cicero, Xenophon, Homer, were veiled and misty experiences to him. His mind was a moving present, obliterating each day what it had read the day before, and piercing into a no more comprehended future. He could at no time have given any intelligible account of Æneas's wanderings or what Cicero was really inveighing against. The Iliad was even more obscure. The only thing which impressed him deeply was an expurgated passage, which he looked up somewhere else and found to be about Mars and Venus caught in the golden bed. Cæsar seemed to be at war, and Xenophon wandering somewhere in Asia Minor, with about the same lengthiness and hardship as Miro suffered in reading him. The trouble, Miro thought afterwards, was that these books were to his mind flickering lights in a vast jungle of ignorance. He does not remember marvelling at the excessive dullness of the stories themselves. He plodded his faithful way, using them as his conscientious teachers did, as exercises in language. He looked on Virgil and Cicero as essentially problems in disentangling words which had unaccountably gotten into a bizarre order, and in recognizing certain rather amusing and ingenious combinations, known as "constructions." Why these words took so irritating an order Miro never knew, but he always connected the problem with those algebraic puzzles he had elsewhere to unravel. Virgil's words were further complicated by being arranged in lines which one had to "scan." Miro was pleased with the rhythm, and there were stanzas that had a roll of their own. But the inexorable translating that had to go on tore all this fabric of poetry to pieces. His translations were impeccable, but, as he never wrote them down, he had never before his eyes the consecutive story.

Translations Miro never saw. He knew that they were implements of deadly sin that boys used to cheat with. His horror of them was such as a saint might feel towards a parody of the Bible. Just before Miro left school, his sister in a younger class began to read a prose translation of the Odyssey, and Miro remembers the scorn with which he looked down on so sneaking an entrance into the temple of light. He knew that not everyone could study Latin and Greek, and he learned to be proud of his knowledge. When at last he had passed his examinations for college—his Latin composition and grammar, his syntax and his sight-reading, and his Greek composition and grammar, his Greek syntax and sight-reading, and his translation of Gallic battles and Anabatic frosts, and Dido's farewell and Cicero's objurgations—his zealous rage did not abate. He even insisted on reading the Bucolics, while he was away on his vacation, and a book or two in the Odyssey. His family was a little chilled by his studiousness, but he knew well that he was laying up cultural treasures in heaven, where moth and rust do not corrupt, neither do thieves break in and steal.

Arrived at college, Miro expanded his cultural interests on the approved lines. He read Horace and Plato, Lysias and Terence, impartially, with faithful conscience. Horace was the most exciting because of the parodies that were beginning to appear in the cleverer newspapers. Miro scarcely knew whether to be amused or shocked at "Odi Persicos" or "Integer Vitæ" done into current slang. The professors, mild-mannered men who knew their place and kept it, never mentioned these impudent adventures, but for Miro it was the first crack in his Ptolemaic system of reverences. There came a time when his mind began to feel replete, when this heavy pushing through the opaque medium of dead language began to fatigue him. He should have been able to read fluently, but there were always turning up new styles, new constructions, to plague him. Latin became to him like a constant diet of beefsteak, and Greek like a constant diet of fine wheaten bread. They lost their taste. These witty poets and ostentatious orators—what were they all about? What was their background? Where did they fit into Miro's life? The professors knew some history, but what did that history mean? Miro found himself surfeited and dissatisfied. He began to look furtively at translations to get some better English than he was able to provide. The hair-splittings of Plato began to bore him when he saw them in crystal-clear English, and not muffled in the original Greek. His apostasy had begun.

It was not much better in his study of English literature. Miro was given a huge anthology, a sort of press-clipping bureau of *belles-lettres*, from Chaucer to Arthur Symons. Under the direction of a professor who was laying out a career for himself as poet—or "modern singer," as he expressed it—the class went briskly through the centuries sampling their genius and tasting the various literary flavors. The enterprise reminded Miro of those books of woollen samples which one looks through when one is to have a suit of clothes made. But in this case, the student did not even have the pleasure of seeing the suit of clothes. All that was expected of him, apparently, was that he should become familiar, from these microscopic pieces, with the different textures and patterns. The great writers passed before his mind like figures in a crowded street. There was no time for preferences. Indeed the professor strove diligently to give each writer his just due. How was one to appreciate the great thoughts and the great styles if one began to choose violently between them, or attempt any discrimination on grounds of their peculiar congeniality for one's own soul? Criticism had to spurn such subjectivity, scholarship could not be wilful. The neatly arranged book of "readings," with its medicinal doses of inspiration, became the symbol of Miro's education.

These early years of college did not deprive Miro of his cultural loyalty, but they deadened his appetite. Al-

27

though almost inconceivably docile, he found himself being bored. He had come from school a serious boy, with more than a touch of priggishness in him, and a vague aspiration to be a "man of letters." He found himself becoming a collector of literary odds-and-ends. If he did not formulate this feeling clearly, he at least knew. He found that the literary life was not as interesting as he had expected. He sought no adventures. When he wrote, it was graceful lyrics of polite criticisms of William Collins or Charles Lamb. These canonized saints of culture still held the field for Miro, however. There was nothing between them and that popular literature of the day that all good men bemoaned. Classic or popular, "highbrow" or "lowbrow," this was the choice, and Miro unquestioningly took the orthodox heaven. In 1912 the most popular of Miro's English professors had never heard of Galsworthy, and another was creating a flurry of scandal in the department by recommending Chesterton to his classes. It would scarcely have been in college that Miro would have learned of an escape from the closed dichotomy of culture. Bored with the "classic," and frozen with horror at the "popular," his career as a man of culture must have come to a dragging end if he had not been suddenly liberated by a chance lecture which he happened to hear while he was at home for the holidays.

The literary radical who appeared before the Lyceum Club of Miro's village was none other than Professor William Lyon Phelps, and it is to that evening of cultural audacity Miro thinks he owes all his later emancipation.

The lecturer grappled with the "modern novel," and tossed Hardy, Tolstoi, Turgenev, Meredith, even Trollope, into the minds of the charmed audience with such effect that the virgin shelves of the village library were ravished for days to come by the eager minds upon whom these great names dawned for the first time. "Jude the Obscure" and "Resurrection" were of course kept officially away from the vulgar, but Miro managed to find "Smoke" and "Virgin Soil" and "Anna Karenina" and "The Warden" and "A Pair of Blue Eyes" and "The Return of the Native." Later at college he explored the forbidden realms. It was as if some devout and restless saint had suddenly been introduced to the Apocrypha. A new world was opened to Miro that was neither "classic" nor "popular," and yet which came to one under the most unimpeachable auspices. There was, at first, it is true, an air of illicit adventure about the enterprise. The lecturer who made himself the missionary of such vigorous and piquant doctrine had the air of being a heretic, or at least a boy playing out of school. But Miro himself returned to college a cultural revolutionist. His orthodoxies crumbled. He did not try to reconcile the new with the old. He applied pick and dynamite to the whole structure of the canon. Irony, humor, tragedy, sensuality, suddenly appeared to him as literary qualities in forms that he could understand. They were like oxygen to his soul.

If these qualities were in the books he had been reading, he had never felt them. The expurgated sample-books he had studied had passed too swiftly over the Elizabethans to give him a sense of their lustiness. Miro immersed himself voluptuously in the pessimism of Hardy. He fed on the poignant torture of Tolstoi. While he was reading "Resurrection," his class in literature was making an "intensive" study of Tennyson. It was too much. Miro rose in revolt. He forswore literary courses forever, dead rituals in which anaemic priests mumbled their trite critical commentary. Miro did not know that to naughtier critics even Mr. Phelps might eventually seem a pale and timid Gideon, himself stuck in moral sloughs. He was grateful enough for that blast of trumpets which made his own scholastic walls fall down.

The next stage in Miro's cultural life was one of frank revolt. He became as violent as a heretic as he had been docile as a believer. Modern novels merely started the rift that widened into modern ideas. The professors were of little use. Indeed, when Miro joined a group of radicals who had started a new college paper, a relentless vendetta began with the teachers. Miro and his friends threw over everything that was mere literature. Social purpose must shine from any writing that was to rouse their enthusiasm. Literary flavor was to be permissiblt only where it made vivid high and revolutionary thought. Tolstoi became their god, Wells their high priest. Chesterton infuriated them. They wrote violent assaults upon him which began in imitation of his cool paradoxicality and ended in incoherent ravings. There were so many enemies to their new fervor that they scarcely knew where to begin. There were not only the old tables of stone to destroy, but there were new and threatening prophets of the eternal verities who had to be exposed. The nineteenth century which they had studied must be weeded of its nauseous moralists. The instructors consulted together how they might put down the revolt, and bring these sinners back to the faith of cultural scripture.

It was of no avail. In a short time Miro had been converted from an aspiration for the career of a cultivated "man of letters" to a fiery zeal for artistic and literary propaganda in the service of radical ideas. One of the results of this conversion was the discovery that he really had no standards of critical taste. Miro had been reverential so long that he had felt no preferences. Everything that was classic had to be good to him. But now that he had thrown away the books that were stamped with the mark of the classic mint, and was dealing with the raw materials of letters, he had to become a critic and make selection. It was not enough that a book should be radical. Some of the books he read, though impeccably revolutionary as to ideas, were clearly poor as literature. His muffled taste began to assert itself. He found himself impressionable where before he had been only mildly acquisitive. The literature of revolt and free speculation fired him into a state of spiritual explosiveness. All that he read now stood out in brighter colors and in sharper outlines than before. As he reached a better balance, he began to feel the vigor of literary form, the value of sincerity and freshness of style. He began to look for them keenly in everything he read. It was long before Miro realized that enthusiasm not docility had made him critical. He became a little proud of his sensitive and discriminating reactions to the modern and the unsifted.

This pursuit had to take place without any help from the college. After Miro graduated, it is true that it became the fashion to study literature as the record of ideas and not merely as a canon of sacred books to be analyzed, commented upon, and absorbed. But no dent was made upon the system in Miro's time, and, the inventory of English criticism not going beyond Stevenson, no college course went beyond Stevenson. The Elizabethans had been exhumed and fumigated, but the most popular attention went to the gallery of Victorians, who combined moral soundness with literary beauty, and were therefore considered wholesome food for young men. The instructors all remained in the state of reverence which saw all things good that had been immemorially taught. Miro's own teacher was a fragile, earnest young man, whose robuster parents had evidently seized upon his nature as a fortunate pledge of what the family might produce in the way of an intellectual flower that should surpass in culture and gentility the ambitions of his parents. His studiousness, hopeless for his father's career as grocer, had therefore been capitalized into education.

The product now shone forth as one of the most successful and promising younger instructors in the department. He knew his subject. Card-indexes filled his room, covering in detail the works, lives, and deaths of the illustrious persons whom he expounded, as well as everything that had been said about them in the way of appreciation or interpretation. An endless number of lectures and courses could be made from this bountiful store. He never tried to write himself, but he knew all about the different kinds of writing, and when he corrected the boys' themes he knew infallibly what to tell them to avoid. Miro's vagaries scandalized his teacher all the more because during his first year in college Miro had been generally noticed as one with the proper sobriety and scholarly patience to graduate into a similar priestly calling. Miro found scant sympathy in the young man. To the latter, literary studies were a science not an art, and they were to be treated with somewhat the same cold rigor of delimitation and analysis as any other science. Miro felt his teacher's recoil at the idea that literature was significant only as the expression of personality or as interpretation of some social movement. Miro saw how uneasy he became when he was confronted with current literature. It was clear that Miro's slowly growing critical sense had not a counterpart in the scholastic mind.

When Miro and his friends abandoned literary studies, they followed after the teachers of history and philosophy, intellectual arenas of which the literary professors seemed scandalously ignorant. At this ignorance Miro boiled with contempt. Here were the profitable clues that would give meaning to dusty literary scholarship, but the scholars had not the wits to seize them. They lived along, playing what seemed to Miro a rather dreary game, when they were not gaping reverently at ideas and forms which they scarcely had the genuine personality to appreciate. Miro felt once and for all free of these mysteries and reverences. He was to know the world as it has been and as it is. He was to put literature into its proper place, making all "culture" serve its apprenticeship for him as interpretation of things larger than itself, of the course of individual lives and the great tides of society.

Miro's later cultural life is not without interest. When he had finished college and his architectural course, and was making headway in his profession, his philosophy of the intellectual life began to straighten itself out. Rapid as his surrender of orthodoxy had been, it had taken him some time to live down that early education. He found now that he would have to live down his heresies also, and get some coherent system of tastes that was his own and not the fruit of either docility or the zeal of propaganda.

The old battles that were still going on helped Miro to realize his modern position. It was a queer, musty quarrel, but it was enlisting minds from all classes and of all intellectual fibers. The "classics" were dying hard, as Miro recognized whenever he read, in the magazines, attacks on the "new education." He found that professors were still taken seriously who declared in passion that without the universal study of the Latin language in American schools all conceptions of taste, standards, criticism, the historic sense itself, would vanish from the earth. He found that even as late as 1917 professional men were gathering together in solemn conclave and buttressing the "value of the classics" with testimonials from "successful men" in a variety of vocations. Miro was amused at the fact that the mighty studies once pressed upon him so uncritically should now require, like the patent medicines, testimonials as to their virtue. Bank presidents, lawyers, and editors had taken the Latin language regularly for years, and had found its effects painless and invigorating. He could not escape the unconscious satire that such plump and prosperous Americans expressed when they thought it admirable to save their cherished intellectual traditions in any such fashion.

Other conservatives Miro saw to be abandoning the line of opposition to science, only to fall back on the line of a defensive against "pseudo-science," as they seemed to call whatever intellectual interests had not yet become indubitably reputable. It was a line which would hold them rather strongly for a time, Miro thought, because so many of the cultural revolutionists agreed with them in hating some of these arrogant and mechanical psychologies and sociologies that reduced life to figures or organisms. But Miro felt also how obstructive was their fight. If the "classics" had done little for him except to hold his mind in an uncomprehending prison, and fetter his spontaneous taste, they seemed to have done little more for even the thorough scholars. When professors had devoted scholarly lives to the "classics" only to exhibit in their own polemics none of the urbanity and intellectual command which were supposed by the believer somehow to rub off automatically on the faithful student, Miro had to conclude an absence of causal connection between the "classics" and the able modern mind. When, more-over, critical power or creative literary work became al-most extinct among these defenders of the "old educa-tion," Miro felt sure that a revolution was needed in the materials and attitudes of "culture."

The case of the defenders was all the weaker because their enemies were not wanton infidels, ignorant of the holy places they profaned. They were rather cultural "Modernists," reforming the church from within. They had the classic background, these young vandals, but they had escaped from its flat and unoriented surface. Abreast of the newer objective, impersonal standards of thinking, they saw the weakness of these archaic minds which could only appeal to vested interests in culture and testi-monials from successful men.

The older critics had long since disavowed the inten-tion of discriminating among current writers. These men, who had to have an Academy to protect them, lumped the younger writers of verse and prose together as "an-archic" and "naturalistic," and had become, in these latter days, merely peevish and querulous, protesting in favor of standards that no longer represented our best values. Every one, in Miro's time, bemoaned the lack of critics, but the older critics seemed to have lost all sense of hos-pitality and to have become tired and a little spitefully disconsolate, while the newer ones were too intent on their crusades against puritanism and philistinism to have time for a constructive pointing of the way.

Miro had a very real sense of standing at the end of an

era. He and his friends had lived down both their old orthodoxies of the classics and their new orthodoxies of propaganda. Gone were the priggishness and self-consciousness which had marked their teachers. The new culture would be more personal than the old, but it would not be held as a personal property. It would be democratic in the sense that it would represent each person's honest spontaneous taste. The old attitude was only speciously democratic. The assumption was that if you pressed your material long enough and winningly enough upon your culturable public, they would acquire it. But the material was sometimes handed down, not grown in the garden of their own appreciations. Under these conditions the critic and appreciator became a mere impersonal register of orthodox opinion. The cultivated person, in confronting his judgments to what was authoritatively taught him, was really a member of the herd—a cultivated herd, it is true, but still a herd. It was the mass that spoke through the critic and not his own discrimination. These authoritative judgments might, of course, have come—probably had come—to the herd through discerning critics, but in Miro's time judgment in the schools had petrified. One believed not because one felt the original discernment, but because one was impressed by the weight and reputability of opinion. At least so it seemed to Miro.

Now just as the artists had become tired of conventions and were breaking through into new and personal forms, so Miro saw the younger critics breaking through these cultural conventions. To the elders the result would seem mere anarchy. But Miro's attitude did not want to destroy, it merely wanted to rearrange the materials. He wanted no more second-hand appreciations. No one's cultural store was to include anything that one could not be enthusiastic about. One's acquaintance with the best that had been said and thought should be encouraged—in Miro's ideal school—to follow the lines of one's temperament. Miro, having thrown out the old gods, found them slowly and properly coming back to him. Some would always repel him, others he hoped to understand eventually. But if it took wisdom to write the great books, did it not also take wisdom to understand them? Even the Latin writers he hoped to recover, with the aid of translations. But why bother with Greek when you could get Euripides in the marvellous verse of Gilbert Murray? Miro was willing to believe that no education was complete without at least an inoculation of the virus of the two orthodoxies that he was transcending.

As Miro looked around the American scene, he wondered where the critics were to come from. He saw, on the one hand, Mr. Mencken and Mr. Dreiser and their friends, going heavily forth to battle with the Philistines, glorying in pachydermatous vulgarisms that hurt the polite and cultivated young men of the old school. And he saw these violent critics, in their rage against puritanism, becoming themselves moralists, with the same bigotry and tastelessness as their enemies. No, these would never do. On the other hand, he saw Mr. Stuart P. Sherman, in

his youthful if somewhat belated ardor, revolting so conscientiously against the "naturalism" and crude expression
of current efforts that, in his defense of *belles-lettres*, of
the fine tradition of literary art, he himself became a
moralist of the intensest brand, and as critic plumped for
Arnold Bennett, because that clever man had a feeling
for the proprieties of human conduct. No, Mr. Sherman
would do even less adequately. His fine sympathies were
as much out of the current as was the specious classicism
of Professor Shorey. He would have to look for the critics
among the young men who had an abounding sense of
life, as well as a feeling for literary form. They would
be men who had not been content to live on their cultural
inheritance, but had gone out into the modern world and
amassed a fresh fortune of their own. They would be
men who were not squeamish, who did not feel the delicate differences between "animal" and "human" conduct,
who were enthusiastic about Mark Twain and Gorki as
well as Romain Rolland, and at the same time were thrilled
by Copeau's theater.

Where was a better program for culture, for any kind
of literary art? Culture as a living effort, a driving attempt
both at sincere expression and at the comprehension of
sincere expression wherever it was found! Appreciation
to be as far removed from the "I know what I like!" as
from the textbook impeccability of taste! If each mind
sought its own along these lines, would not many find
themselves agreed? Miro insisted on liking Amy Lowell's
attempt to outline the tendencies in American poetry in

a form which made clear the struggles of contemporary men and women with the tradition and against "every affectation of the mind." He began to see in the new class-consciousness of poets the ending of that old division which "culture" made between the chosen people and the gentiles. We were now to form little pools of workers and appreciators of similar temperaments and tastes. The little magazines that were starting up became voices for these new communities of sentiment. Miro thought that perhaps at first it was right to adopt a tentative supercili-ousness towards the rest of the world, so that both Mr. Mencken with his shudders at the vulgar Demos and Mr. Sherman with his obsession with the sanely and whole-somely American might be shut out from influence. In-stead of fighting the Philistine in the name of freedom, or fighting the vulgar iconoclast in the name of whole-some human notions, it might be better to write for one's own band of comprehenders, in order that one might have something genuine with which to appeal to both the mob of the "bourgeois" and the ferocious vandals who had been dividing the field among them. Far better a quarrel among these intensely self-conscious groups than the issues that had filled *The Atlantic* and *The Na-tion* with their dreary obsolescence. Far better for the mind that aspired towards "culture" to be told not to con-form or worship, but to search out its group, its own tem-peramental community of sentiment, and there deepen appreciations through sympathetic contact.

It was no longer a question of being hospitable towards

the work of other countries. Miro found the whole world open to him, in these days, through the enterprise of publishers. He and his friends felt more sympathetic with certain groups in France and Russia than they did with the variegated "prominent authors" of their own land. Winston Churchill as a novelist came to seem more of an alien than Artzybashev. The fact of culture being international had been followed by a sense of its being. The old cultural attitude had been hospitable enough, but it had imported its alien culture in the form of "comparative literature." It was hospitable only in trying to mould its own taste to the orthodox canons abroad. The older American critic was mostly interested in getting the proper rank and reverence for what he borrowed. The new critic will take what suits his community of sentiment. He will want to link up not with the foreign canon, but with that group which is nearest in spirit with the effort he and his friends are making. The American has to work to interpret and portray the life he knows. He cannot be international in the sense that anything but the life in which he is saturated, with its questions and its colors, can be the material for his art. But he can be international—and must be—in the sense that he works with a certain hopeful vision of a "young world," and with certain ideal values upon which the younger men, stained and revolted by war, in all countries are agreeing.

Miro wonders sometimes whether the direction in which he is tending will not bring him around the circle again to a new classicism. The last stage in the history of the man of culture will be that "classic" which he did not understand and which his mind spent its youth in overthrowing. But it will be a classicism far different from that which was so unintelligently handed down to him in the American world. It will be something worked out and lived into. Looking into the future he will have to do what Van Wyck Brooks calls "inventing a usable past." Finding little in the American tradition that is not tainted with sweetness and light and burdened with the terrible patronage of bourgeois society, the new classicist will yet rescue Thoreau and Whitman and Mark Twain and try to tap through them a certain eternal human tradition of abounding vitality and moral freedom, and so build out the future. If the classic means power with restraint, vitality with harmony, a fusion of intellect and feeling, and a keen sense of the artistic conscience, then the revolutionary world is coming out into the classic. When Miro sees behind the minds of *The Masses* group a desire for form and for expressive beauty, and sees the radicals following Jacques Copeau and reading Chekhov, he smiles at the thought of the American critics, young and old, who do not know yet that they are dead.

Mon Amie

S H E   W A S   F R E N C H   from the crown of her head to
the soles of her feet, but she was of that France which few
Americans, I think, know or imagine. She belonged to
that France which Jean-Christophe found in his friend
Olivier, a world of flashing ideas and enthusiasms, a
golden youth of ideals.

She had picked me out for an exchange of conversation,
as the custom is, precisely because I had left my name at
the Sorbonne as a person who wrote a little. I had put this
bait out, as it were, deliberately, with the intention of
hooking a mind that cared for a little more than mere
chatter, but I had hardly expected to find it in the form
of a young girl who, as she told me in her charmingly
polished note, was nineteen and had just completed her
studies.

These studies formed a useful introduction when she
received me in the little old-fashioned apartment in the
Batignolles quarter on my first visit. She had made them
ever since she was five years old in a wonderful old convent at Bourges; and in the town had lived her grandmother, a very old lady, whom she had gone lovingly to
see, as often as she could be away from the watchful care
of the nuns. In her she had found her real mother, for her

parents had been far away in Brittany. When the old lady died, my friend had to face an empty world, and to become acquainted all over again with a mother whom she confessed she found "little sympathetic." But she was a girl of *devoir*, and she would do nothing to wound her.

She told me one afternoon as we took our first walk through the dusky richness of the Musée Cluny, that the shock of death had disclosed to her how fleeting life was, how much she thought of death, and how much she feared it. I used the lustiness of her grandmother's eighty-four years to convince her as to how long she might have to postpone her dread, but her fragile youth seemed already to feel the beating wings about her. As she talked, her expression had all that wistful seriousness of the French face which has not been devitalized by the city, that sense of the nearness of unutterable things which runs, a golden thread, through their poetry. Though she had lived away from Brittany, in her graver moments there was much in her of the patient melancholy of the Breton. For her father's people had been seafolk,—not fishermen, but pilots and navigators on those misty and niggardly shores,—and the long defeat and ever-trustful suffering was in her blood. She would interpret to me the homely pictures at the Luxembourg which spoke of coast and peasant life; and her beautiful articulateness brought the very soul of France out of the canvases of Cottet and Breton and Carrière. She understood these people.

But she was very various, and, if at first we plumbed together the profoundest depths of her, we soon got into shallower waters. The fluency of her thought outran any foreign medium, and made anything but her flying French impossible. Her meager English had been learned from some curious foreigner with an accent more German than French, and we abandoned it by mutual consent. Our conversation became an exchange of ideas and not of languages. Or rather her mind became the field where I explored at will.

I think I began by assuming a Catholic devotion in her, and implied that her serious outlook on life might lead her into the church. She scoffed unmitigatedly at this. The nuns were not unkindly, she said, but they were hard and narrow and did not care for the theater and for books, which she adored.

She believed in God. "Et le théâtre!" I said, which delighted her hugely. But these Christian virtues made unlovely characters and cut one off so painfully from the fascinating moving world of ideas outside. But surely after fourteen years of religious training and Christian care, did she not believe in the Church, its priesthood and its dogmas?

She repudiated her faith with indescribable vivacity. A hardened Anglo-Saxon agnostic would have shown more diffidence in denying his belief in dogma or the Bible. As for the latter, she said, it might do for children of five years. And the cutting sweep of that "enfants de cinq ans" afforded me a revealing glimpse of that lucid intelligence with which the French mind cuts through layers and strata of equivocation and compromise.

45

Most Frenchmen, if they lose their faith, go the swift and logical road to atheism. Her loss was no childish dream or frenzy; she still believed in God. But as for the Church and its priesthood,—she told me, with malicious irony, and with the intelligence that erases squeamishness, of a friend of hers who was the daughter of the priest in charge of one of the largest Parisian churches. Would she confess to a member of a priestly caste which thus broke faith? Confession was odious anyway. She had been kept busy in school inventing sins. She would go to church on Easter, but she would not take the Eucharist, though I noticed a charming lapse when she crossed herself with holy water as we entered Notre Dame one day.

Where had she ever got such ideas, shut up in a convent?—Oh, they were all perfectly obvious, were they not? Where would one not get them? This amazing soul of modern France!—which pervades even the walls of convents with its spirit of free criticism and its terrible play of the intelligence; which will examine and ruthlessly cast aside, just as my vibrant, dark-haired, fragile friend was casting aside, without hypocrisy or scruple, whatever ideas do not seem to enhance the clear life to be lived.

II

Accustomed to grope and flounder in the mazes of the intellect, I found her intelligence well-nigh terrifying. I would sit almost helplessly and listen to her sparkle of talk. Her freedom knocked into pieces all my little imagined world of French conventionalities and inhibitions. How could this pale, dignified mother, to whom I was presented as she passed hurriedly through the room one day, allow her to wander so freely about Paris parks and museums with a foreign young man? Her answer came superbly, with a flare of decision which showed me that at least in one spot the eternal conflict of the generations had been settled: *"Je me permets!"*—I allow myself. She gave me to understand that for a while her mother had been difficult, but that there was no longer any question of her "living her life"—*vivre sa vie*. And she really thought that her mother, in releasing her from the useless trammels, had become herself much more of an independent personality. As for my friend, she dared, she took risks, she played with the adventure of life. But she knew what was there.

The motherly Anglo-Saxon frame of mind would come upon me, to see her in the light of a poor ignorant child, filled with fantastic ideals, all so pitifully untested by experience. How ignorant she was of life, and to what pitfalls her daring freedom must expose her in this unregenerate France! I tried and gave it up. As she talked,—her glowing eyes, in which ideas seemed to well up brimming with feeling and purpose, saying almost more than her words,—she seemed too palpably a symbol of luminous youth, a flaming militant of the younger generation, who by her courage would shrivel up the dangers that so beset the timorous. She was French, and that fact by itself meant that whole layers of equivocation had been cut through, whole sets of intricacies avoided.

In order to get the full shock of her individuality, I took her one afternoon to a model little English tea-room on the rue de Rivoli, where normal Britishers were reading *Punch* and the *Spectator* over their jam and cake. The little flurry of disapprobation and the hostile stare which our appearance elicited from the well-bred families and discreet young men at the tables, the flaring incongruity of her dark, lithe, inscrutable personality in this bland, vacuous British atmosphere, showed me as could nothing else how hard was the gem-like flame with which she burned.

As we walked in the Luxembourg and along the quays, or sat on the iron chairs in the gardens of the Parc Monceau or the Trocadéro, our friendship became a sort of intellectual orgy. The difficulty of following the pace of her flying tongue and of hammering and beating my own thoughts into the unaccustomed French was fatiguing, but it was the fascinating weariness of exploration. My first idle remarks about God touched off a whole battery of modern ideas. None of the social currents of the day seemed to have passed her by, though she had been immured so long in her sleepy convent at Bourges. She had that same interest and curiosity about other classes and conditions of life which animates us here in America, and the same desire to do something effective against the misery of poverty.

I had teased her a little about her academic, untried

ideas, and in grave reproof she told me, one afternoon, as we stood—of all places!—on the porch of the Little Trianon at Versailles, a touching story of a family of the poorest of the Parisian poor, whom she and her mother visited and helped to get work. She did not think charity accomplished very much, and flamed at the word "Socialism," although she had not yet had its program made very clear to her.

But mostly she was feminist,—an ardent disciple in that singularly uncomplicated and happy march of the Frenchwomen, already so practically emancipated, toward a definite social recognition of that liberation. The normal Frenchwoman, in all but the richer classes, is an economic asset to her country. And economic independence was a cardinal dogma in my friend's faith. She was already taking a secretarial course, in order to ensure her ability to make her living; and she looked forward quite eagerly to a career.

Marriage was in considerable disfavor; it had still the taint of the Church upon it, while the civil marriage seemed, with the only recently surrendered necessary parental consent, to mark the subjection of the younger to the older generation. These barriers were now removed, but the evil savor of the institution lingered on. My friend, like all the French intellectuals, was all for the "union libre," but it would have to be loyal unto death. It was all the more inspiring as an ideal, because it would be perhaps hard to obtain. Men, she was inclined to think, were usually *malhonnête*, but she might find some

49

day a man of complete sympathy and complete loyalty. But she did not care. Life was life, freedom was freedom, and the glory of being a woman in the modern world was enough for her.

The French situation was perhaps quite as bad it it was pictured. Friendship between a girl and a young man was almost impossible. It was that they usually wished to love her. She did not mind them on the streets. The students—oh, the students!—were frightfully annoying; but perhaps one gave a *gifle* and passed rapidly on. Her parents, before she had become genuinely the captain of her soul, had tried to marry her off in the orthodox French way. She had had four proposals. Risking the clean candor of the French soul, I became curious and audacious. So she dramatized for me, without a trace of self-consciousness, a wonderful little scene of provincial manners. The stiff young Frenchman making his stilted offer, her self-possessed reluctance, her final refusal, were given in inimitable style. These incidents, which in the life of a little American *bourgeoise* would have been cries or triumphs, and, at any rate, unutterably hoarded secrets, were given with a cold frankness which showed refreshingly to what insignificance marriage was relegated in her life. She wished, she said, to *vivre sa vie*—to live her life. If marriage fitted in with her living of her life, it might take her. It should never submerge or deflect her. Countless Frenchwomen, in defiance of the strident Anglo-Saxon belief, were able both to keep a household and to earn their own living; and why not she also? She would always be free; and her black eyes burned as they looked out so fearlessly into a world that was to be all hers, because she expected nothing from it.

About this world, she had few illusions. To its worldliness and glitter she showed really a superb indifference. I brutally tried to trap her into a confession that she spurned it only because it might be closed to her through lack of money or prestige. Her eloquent eyes almost slew me with vivacious denial. She despised these "dolls" whose only business in life was to wear clothes. Her own sober black was not affectation, but only her way of showing that she was more than a *poupée*. She did not say it, but I quite appreciated, and I knew well that she knew, how charming a *poupée* she might have made.

Several of her friends were gay and worldly. She spoke of them with charming frankness, touching off, with a tone quite clean of malice, all their little worthlessnesses and futilities. Some of this world, indeed, shaded off into unimaginable *nuances*, but she was wholly aware of its significance. In the inimitable French way, she disdained to use its errors as a lever to elevate her own virtues.

III

Her blazing candor lighted up for me every part of her world. We skirted abysses, but the language helped us wonderfully through. French has worn tracks in so many fields of experience where English blunders either boorishly or sentimentally. French is made for illumination and clear expression; it has kept its purity and crispness and can express, without shamefacedness or bungling, attitudes and interpretations which the Anglo-Saxon fatuously hides.

My friend was dimly sensible of some such contrast. I think she had as much difficulty in making me out as I had in making her out. She was very curious as to how she compared with American girls. She had once met one but had found her, though not a doll, yet not *sympathique* and little understandable. I had to tell my friend how untranslatable she was. The Anglo-Saxon, I had to tell her, was apt to be either a school-child or a middle-aged person. To the first, ideas were strange and disturbing. To the second, they were a nuisance and a bore. I almost assured her that in America she would be considered a quite horrible portent. Her brimming idealism would make everybody uncomfortable. The sensual delight which she took in thinking, the way her ideas were all warmly felt and her feelings luminously expressed, would adapt her badly to a world of school-children and tired business men. I tried to go over for her the girls of her age whom I had known. How charming they were to be sure, but, even when they had ideas, how strangely inarticulate they sometimes were, and, if they were articulate, how pedantic and priggish they seemed to the world about them! And what forests of reticences and exaggerated values there were, and curious illogicalities. How jealous they were of their personalities, and what a suspicious and individualistic guard they kept over their candor and sincerities! I was very gay and perhaps a little cruel.

She listened eagerly, but I think she did not quite understand. If one were not frankly a doll, was not life a great swirl to be grappled with and clarified, and thought and felt about? And as for her personality, the more she gave the more she had. She would take the high risks of friendship.

To cross the seas and come upon my own enthusiasms and ideals vibrating with so intense a glow seemed an amazing fortune. It was like coming upon the same design, tinted in novel and picturesque colors of a finer harmony. In this intellectual flirtation, carried on in *musée* and garden and on quay throughout that cloudless April, I began to suspect some gigantic flattery. Was her enthusiasm sincere, and her clean-cutting ideas, or had she by some subtle intuition anticipated me? Did she think, or was it to be expected of me, that I should fall in love with her? But perhaps there was a touch of the too foreign in her personality. And if I had fallen in love, I know it would not have been with herself. It would have been with the Frenchness of her, and perhaps was. It would have been with the eternal youth of France that she was. For she could never have been so very glowing if France had not been full of her. Her charm and appeal were far broader than herself. It took in all that rare spiritual climate where one absorbs ideas and ideals as the earth drinks in rain.

She was of that young France with its luminous understanding, its personal verve, its light of expression, its way of feeling its ideas and thinking its emotions, its deathless loyalty which betrays only at the clutch of some deeper loyalty. She adored her country and all its mystic values and aspirations. When she heard I was going to Germany, she actually winced with pain. She could scarcely believe it. I fell back at once to the position of a vulgar traveler, visiting even the lands of the barbarians. They were her country's enemies, and some day they would attack. France awaited the onslaught fatalistically. She did not want to be a man, but she wished that they would let women be soldiers. If the war came, however, she would enlist at once as a Red Cross nurse. She thrilled at the thought that perhaps there she could serve to the uttermost.

And the war has come, hot upon her enthusiasms. She must have been long since in the field, either at the army stations, or moving about among the hospitals of Paris, her heart full of pride and pity for the France which she loved and felt so well, and of whose deathless spirit she was, for me, at least, so glowing a symbol.

Fergus

MY FRIEND FERGUS has all the characteristics of
genius except the divine fire. The guardian angel who
presided at his birth and set in order all his delicate appreciations just forgot to start flowing the creative current.
Fergus was born to suffer the pangs of artistic desire
without the gushing energy that would have moulded artistic form. It was perhaps difficult enough to produce
him as it was. There is much that is clearly impossible
about him. His father is a bluff old Irish newspaper com-
positor, with the obstinately genial air of a man who cannot believe that life will not some day do something for
him. His mother is a French-Canadian, jolly and stout,
who plays old Irish and French melodies on the harp,
and mothers the young Catholic girls of the crowded city
neighborhood in which they live. She has the slightly
surprised background of never realized prosperity. Fergus is an old child, and moves in the dark little flat, with
its green plush furniture, its prints of the Great Com-
moner and Lake Killarney, its Bible texts of the Holy
Name, with the detached condescension of an exiled
prince. He is very dark and finely formed, of the type

that would be taken for a Spaniard in France and an Italian in Spain, and his manners have the distinction of the born aristocrat.

The influences of that close little Catholic society in which he was brought up he has shed as a duck sheds water. His mother wished him to be a Jesuit. The quickness of his mind, the refinement and hauteur of his manner, intoxicated her with the assurance of his priestly future. His father, however, inclined towards the insurance business. Fergus himself viewed his future with cold disinterestedness. When I first met him he had just emerged from a year of violin study at a music school. The violin had been an escape from the twin horrors that had menaced him. On his parents' anxiety that he "make something of himself" he looked with some disdain. He did, however, feel to a certain extent their chagrin at finding so curious and aristocratic a person in their family, and he allowed himself, with a fine stoicism as of an exiled prince supporting himself until the revolution was crushed and he was reinstated in his possessions, to be buried in an insurance broker's office. At this time he spent his evenings in the dim vaulted reading-room of a public library composing music, or in wandering in the park with his friends, discussing philosophy. His little music notebook and Gomperz's "Greek Thinkers" were rarely out of his hand.

Harmony and counterpoint had not appealed to him at the Conservatory, but now the themes that raced and rocketed through his head compelled him to composition. The bloodless scherzos and allegros which he produced and tried to play for me on his rickety piano had so archaic a flavor as to suggest that Fergus was inventing anew the art of music, somewhat as our childhood is supposed to pass through all the stages of the evolution of the race. As he did not seem to pass beyond a pre-Bachian stage, he began to feel at length, he told me, that there was something lacking in his style. But he was afraid that routine study would dull his inspiration. It was time that he needed, and not instruction. And time was slipping so quickly away. He was twenty-two, and he could not grasp or control it.

When summer was near he came to me with an idea. His office work was insupportable. Even accepting that one dropped eight of the best hours of one's every day into a black and bottomless pit in exchange for the privilege of remaining alive, such a life was almost worse than none. I had friends who were struggling with a large country farm. He wished to offer them his services as farmhand on half-time in exchange for simple board and lodging. Working in the morning, he would have all the rest of his pastoral day for writing music.

Before I could communicate to him my friends' reluctance to this proposal, he told me that his musical inspiration had entirely left him. He was now spending all his spare time in the Art Museum, discovering tastes and delights that he had not known were in him. Why had not some one told him of the joy of sitting and reading Plato in those glowing rooms? The Museum was more significant when I walked in it with Fergus. His gracious bearing almost seemed to please the pictures themselves. He walked as a princely connoisseur through his own historic galleries.

When I saw Fergus next, however, a physical depression had fallen upon him. He had gone into a vegetarian diet and was enfeebling himself with Spartan fare. He was disturbed by loneliness, the erotic world gnawed persistently at him, and all the Muses seemed to have left him. But in his gloominess, in the fine discrimination with which he analyzed his helplessness, in the noble despair with which he faced an insoluble world, he was more aristocratic than ever. He was not like one who had never attained genius, fame, voluptuous passion, riches, he was rather as one who had been bereft of all these things.

Returning last autumn from a year abroad, during which I had not heard a word of Fergus, I found he had turned himself into a professional violin-teacher. The insurance job had passed out, and for a few weeks he had supported himself by playing the organ in a small Catholic church. There was jugglery with his salary, however, and it annoyed him to be so intimate a figure in a ritual to which he could only refer in irony. Priests whose "will to power" background he analyzed to me with Nietzschean fidelity always repelled him.

He was saved from falling back on the industrious parents who had so strangely borne him by an offer to play the harmonium in the orchestra of a fashionable restaurant. To this opportunity of making eighteen dollars a week he had evidently gone with a new and pleasurable sense of the power of wealth. It was easy, he said, but the heat and the lights, the food and the long evening hours fairly nauseated him, and he gave the work up.

All this time, I gathered, his parents had been restive over a certain economic waste. They seemed to feel that his expensive musical education should be capitalized more profitably. His mother had even deplored his lack of ambition. She had explored and had discovered that one made much money as a "vaudeville act." He had obtained a trial at an Upper Bronx moving-picture vaudeville theater. Fergus told me that the nervous girl who had gone on the stage before him had been cut short in the middle of her "Fox-Trot Lullaby," or whatever her song was, by hostile yells from the audience. Fergus himself went on in rather a depressed mood, and hardly did himself justice. He played the Bach air, and a short movement from Brahms. He did not, however, get that rapport with his audience which he felt the successful vaudeville artist should feel. They had not yelled at him, but they had refused to applaud, and the circuit manager had declined to engage him.

After this experience it occurred to Fergus that he liked to teach, and that his training had made him a professional musician. His personality, he felt, was not unfavorable. By beginning modestly he saw no reason why he should not build up a clientele and an honorable competence. When I saw him a week later at the Music Settlement, he told me that there was no longer any doubt that he had found his lifework. His fees are very small and his pupils are exacting. He has practised much besides. He told me the other day that teaching was uninspiring drudgery. He had decided to give it up, and compose songs.

Whenever I see Fergus I have a slight quickening of the sense of life. His rich and rather somber personality makes all ordinary backgrounds tawdry. He knows so exactly what he is doing and what he is feeling. I do not think he reads very much, but he breathes in the air around him certain large aethestic and philosophical ideas. There are many philosophies and many artists, however, that he never heard of and this ignorance of the concrete gives one a fine pleasure of impressing him. One can pour into receptive ears judgments and enthusiasms that have long ago been taken for granted by one's more sophisticated friends. His taste in art as in music is impeccable, and veers strongly to the classics—Rembrandt and the Greeks, as Bach and Beethoven.

Fergus has been in love, but he does not talk much about it. A girl in his words is somewhat dark and inscrutable. She always has something haunting and finely-toned about her, whoever she may be. I always think of the clothed lady in the flowing silks, in Titian's "Sacred and Profane Love." Yet withal Fergus gives her a touch of the allurement of her nude companion. His reserve, I think, always keeps these persons very dusky and distant. His chastity is a result of his fineness of taste rather than of feeble desire or conscious control. That impersonal passion which descends on people like Fergus in a sultry cloud he tells me he contrives to work off into his violin. I sometimes wonder if a little more of it with a better violin would have made him an artist.

But destiny has just clipped his wings so that he must live a life of noble leisure instead of artistic creation. His unconscious interest is the art of life. Against a background of Harlem flats and stodgy bourgeois prejudices he works out this life of *otium cum dignitate*, calm speculation and artistic appreciation that Nietzsche glorifies. On any code that would judge him by the seven dollars a week which is perhaps his average income he looks with cold disdain. He does not demand that the world give him a living. He did not ask to come into it, but being here he will take it with candor. Sometimes I think he is very patient with life. Probably he is not happy. This is not important. As his candor and his appreciations refresh me, I wonder if the next best thing to producing works of art is not to be, like Fergus, a work of art one's self.

The Professor

THE PROFESSOR is a young man, but he had so obviously the misfortune of growing up too early that he seems already like a mournful relic of irrevocable days. His ardent youth was spent in that halcyon time of the early nineteen-hundreds when all was innocence in the heart of young America. "When I was in college," the Professor often says, "all this discussion of social questions was unknown to us. The growing seriousness of the American college student is an inspiring phenomenon in our contemporary life."

In those days the young men who felt an urge within them went in for literature. It was still the time when Presbyterian clergymen and courtly Confederate generals were contributing the inspiration of their ripe scholarship to the younger generation. It was the time when Brander Matthews still thrilled the world of criticism with his scintillating Gallic wit and his cosmopolitan wealth of friendships. The younger men of that time are still a race apart. Through these literary masters they touched the intimate life of literature; they knew Kipling and Stevenson, Arthur Symons and the great Frenchmen, and felt themselves one with the charmed literary brotherhood throughout the world. It was still the time when, free from philosophic or sociologic taint, our American youth was privileged to breathe in from men like Henry van Dyke and Charles Eliot Norton the ideals of the scholar and the gentleman.

The Professor's sensitive talent soon asserted itself. With Wordsworth he had absorbed himself into the circumambient life of nature and made the great reconciliation between her and man. With Shelley he had dared unutterable things and beaten his wings against the stars. With Tennyson he had shuddered pensively on the brink of declining faith. With Carlyle he had felt the call of duty, and all the revulsion against a sordid and mechanical age. With Arnold he had sought the sweetness and light which should come to him from knowing all the best that had been said and thought in the world. The Professor had scarcely begun to write verse before he found himself victor in a prize poetry contest which had enlisted the talent of all the best poets of America. He often tells his students of the intoxication of that evening when he encircled the dim vaulted corridors of the college library, while his excited brain beat out the golden couplets of the now celebrated "Ganymede." The success of this undergraduate stripling fell like a thunderbolt upon the literary world. Already consecrated to the scholar's career, he found fallen upon him the miracle of the creative artist. But Shelley and Keats had had their greatness very early, too. And when, at the early age of twenty-three, the Professor published his masterly doctoral dissertation on "The Anonymous Lyrics of the Fourteenth Century," he at once attained in the world of literary scholarship the distinction that "Ganymede" had given him in the world of poetry.

His career has not frustrated those bright promises. His rare fusion of scholarship and genius won him the chair of English Literature in one of our most rapidly growing colleges, where he has incomparable opportunities for influencing the ideals of the young men under him. His courses are among the most popular in the college. Although his special scholarly research has been devoted to pre-Elizabethan literature, he is at home in all the ages. His lectures are models of carefully weighed criticism. "My purpose," he says, "is to give my boys the spirit of the authors, and let them judge between them for themselves." Consequently, however much Swinburne may revolt him, the Professor expounds the carnal and desperate message of that poet with the same care which he gives to his beloved Wordsworth. "When they have heard them all," he told me once, "I can trust my boys to feel the insufficiency of any purely materialistic interpretation of life."

Impeccable as is his critical taste where the classics are concerned, he is reluctant about giving his opinion to those students who come for a clue through the current literary maze. Stevenson was early canonized, and the Professor speaks with charm and fulness upon him, but G. B. S. and Galsworthy must wait. "Time, perhaps,"

64

says the Professor, "will put the seal of approval upon them. Meanwhile our judgment can be only tentative." His fine objectivity is shown in those lists of the hundred best books of the year which he is sometimes asked to compile for the Sunday newspapers. Rarely does a new author, never does a young author, appear among them. Scholarly criticism, the Professor feels, can scarcely be too cautious.

The Professor's inspiring influence upon his students, however, is not confined to his courses. He has formed a little literary society in the college, which meets weekly to discuss with him the larger cultural issues of the time. Lately he has become interested in philosophy. "In my day," he once told me, "we young literary men did not study philosophy." But now, professor that he is, he goes to sit at the feet of the great metaphysicians of his college. He has been immensely stirred by the social moral awakening of recent years. He willingly allows discussions of socialism in his little society, but is inclined to deprecate the fanaticism of college men who lose their sense of proportion on social questions. But in his open-mindedness to radical thought he is an inspiration to all who meet him. To be radical, he tells his boys, is a necessary part of experience. In professorial circles he is looked upon as a veritable revolutionist, for he encourages the discussion of vital questions even in the classroom. Questions such as evolution, capital punishment, free thought, protection and education of women, furnish the themes for composition. And from the essays of the masters—Macaulay,

Huxley, John Stuart Mill and Matthew Arnold—come the great arguments as freshly and as vitally as of yore. Literature, says the Professor, is not merely language; it is ideals. We must above all, he says, teach our undergraduates to think.

Although the Professor is thus responsive to the best radicalism of the day, he does not let their shock break the sacred chalice of the past. He is deeply interested in the religious life of his college. A devout Episcopalian, he deplores the callousness of the present generation towards the immemorial beauty of ritual and dogma. The empty seats of the college chapel fill him with dismay. One of his most beautiful poems pictures his poignant sensations as he comes from a quiet hour within its dim, organ-haunted shadows out into the sunlight, where the careless athletes are running bare-leggedly past him, unmindful of the eternal things.

I think I like the Professor best in his study at home, when he talks on art and life with one or two respectful students. On the wall is a framed autograph of Wordsworth, picked up in some London bookshop; and a framed letter of appreciation from Richard Watson Gilder. On the table stands a richly-bound volume of "Ganymede" with some of the very manuscripts, as he has shown us, bound in among the leaves. His deep and measured voice flows pleasantly on in anecdotes of the Authors' Club, or reminiscences of the golden past. As one listens, the glamor steals upon one. This is the literary life, grave, respected, serene. All else is hectic rush, modern ideas a futile babel. It is men like the Professor who keep the luster of scholarship bright, who hold true the life of the scholar and the gentleman as it was lived of old. In a world of change he keeps the faith pure.

One of Our Conquerors

WHEN Dr. Alexander Mackintosh Butcher was elected
to the presidency of Pluribus University ten years ago,
there was general agreement that in selecting a man who
was not only a distinguished educator but an executive
of marked business ability the trustees had done honor to
themselves and their university as well as to the new
president. For Dr. Butcher had that peculiar genius which
would have made him as successful in Wall Street or in
a governor's chair as in the classroom. Every alumnus of
Pluribus knows the story of the young Alexander Mackintosh Butcher, standing at the age of twenty-two at the
threshold of a career. Eager, energetic, with a brilliant
scholastic record behind him, it was difficult to decide
into what profession he should throw his powerful
talents. To his beloved and aged president the young man
went for counsel. "My boy," said the good old man,
"remember that no profession offers nobler opportunities
for service to humanity than that of education." And
what should he teach? "Philosophy is the noblest study
of man." And a professor of philosophy the young
Butcher speedily became.

Those who were so fortunate as to study philosophy under him at Pluribus will never forget how uncompromisingly he preached absolute idealism, the Good, the True and the Beautiful, or how witheringly he excoriated the mushroom philosophies which were springing up to challenge the eternal verities. I have heard his old students remark the secret anguish which must have been his when later, as president of the university, he was compelled to entertain the famous Swiss philosopher, Monsfilius, whose alluring empiricism was taking the philosophic world by storm.

Dr. Butcher's philosophic acuteness is only equaled by his political rectitude. Indeed, it is as philosopher-politician that he holds the unique place he does in our American life, injecting into the petty issues of the political arena the immutable principles of Truth. Early conscious of his duty as a man and a citizen, he joined the historic party which had earned the eternal allegiance of the nation by rescuing it from slavery. By faithful service to the chiefs of his state organization, first under the powerful Flatt, and later under the well-known Harnes, himself college-bred and a political philosopher of no mean merit, the young Dr. Butcher worked his way up through ward captain to the position of district leader. The practical example of Dr. Butcher, the scholar and educator, leaving the peace of his academic shades to carry the banner in the service of his party ideas of Prosperity and Protection has been an inspiration to thousands of educated men in these days of civic cowardice. When, three years ago, his long and faithful services were rewarded by the honor of second place on the Presidential ticket which swept the great states of Mormonia and Green Mountain, there were none of his friends and admirers who felt that the distinction was undeserved.

President Butcher is frequently called into the councils of the party whenever there are resolutions to be drawn up or statements of philosophic principle to be issued. He is in great demand also as chairman of state conventions, which his rare academic distinction lifts far above the usual level of such affairs. It was at one of these conventions that he made the memorable speech in which he drew the analogy between the immutability of Anglo-Saxon political institutions and the multiplication table. To the applause of the keen and hard-headed business men and lawyers who sat as delegates under him, he scored with matchless satire the idea of progress in politics, and demonstrated to their complete satisfaction that it was as absurd to tinker with the fundamentals of our political system as it would be to construct a new arithmetic. In such characteristic wisdom we have the intellectual caliber of the man.

This brilliant and profound address came only as the fruit of a lifetime of thought on political philosophy. President Butcher's treatise on "Why We Should Never Change Any Form of Government" has been worth more to thoughtful men than thousands of sermons on civic righteousness. No one who has ever heard President Butcher's rotund voice discuss in a public address "those ideas and practices which have been tried and tested by a thousand years of experience" will ever allow his mind to dwell again on the progressive and disintegrating tendencies of the day, nor will he have the heart again to challenge on any subject the "decent respect for the common opinions of mankind."

President Butcher's social philosophy is as sound as his political. The flexibility of his mind is shown in the fact that, although an immutabilist in politics, he is a staunch Darwinian in sociology. Himself triumphantly fit, he never wearies of expressing his robust contempt for the unfit who encumber the earth. His essay on "The Insurrection of the Maladjusted" is already a classic in American literature. The trenchant attack on modern social movements as the impudent revolt of the unfit against those who, by their personal merits and industry, have, like himself, achieved success, has been a grateful bulwark to thousands who might otherwise have been swept sentimentally from their moorings by those false guides who erect their own weakness and failure into a criticism of society.

Dr. Butcher's literary eminence has not only won him a chair in the American Academy of All the Arts, Sciences, and Philosophies, but has made him almost as well known abroad as at home. He has lectured before the learned societies of Lisbon on "The American at Home," and he has a wide circle of acquaintances in every capital in Europe. Most of the foreign universities have awarded him honorary degrees. In spite of his stout Americanism,

Dr. Butcher has one of the most cosmopolitan of minds. His essay on "The Cosmopolitan Intellect" has been translated into every civilized language. With his admired friend, Owen Griffith, he has collaborated in the latter's endeavor to beat the swords of industrial exploitation into the ploughshares of universal peace. He has served in numerous capacities on Griffith's many peace boards and foundations, and has advised him widely and well how to distribute his millions so as to prevent the recurrence of war in future centuries.

Let it not be thought that, in recounting President Butcher's public life and services, I am minimizing his distinction as a university administrator. As executive of one of the largest universities in America, he has raised the position of college president to a dignity surpassed by scarcely any office except President of the United States. The splendid $125,000 mansion which President Butcher had the trustees of Pluribus build for him on the heights overlooking the city, where he entertains distinguished foreign guests with all the pomp worthy of his high office, is the precise measure both of the majesty with which he has endowed the hitherto relatively humble position, and the appreciation of a grateful university. The relations between President Butcher and the trustees of Pluribus have always been of the most beautiful nature. The warm and profound intellectual sympathy which he feels for the methods and practices of the financial and corporate world, and the extensive personal affiliations he has formed with its leaders, have made it possible to leave in his hands a large measure of absolute authority. Huge endowments have made Pluribus under President Butcher's rule one of the wealthiest of our higher institutions of learning. With a rare intuitive response to the spirit of the time, the President has labored to make it the biggest and most comprehensive of its kind. Already its schools are numbered by the dozens, its buildings by the scores, its instructors by the hundreds, its students by the thousands, its income by the millions, and its possessions by the tens of millions.

None who have seen President Butcher in the commencement exercises of Pluribus can ever forget the impressiveness of the spectacle. His resemblance to Henry VIII is more marked now that he has donned the crimson gown and flat hat of the famous English university which gave him the degree of LL.D. Seated in a high-backed chair—the historic chair of the first colonial president of Pluribus—surrounded by tier upon tier of his retinue of the thousand professors of the university, President Alexander Mackintosh Butcher presents the degrees, and in his emphatic voice warns the five thousand graduates before him against everything new, everything untried, everything untested.

Only one office could tempt President Butcher from his high estate. Yet even those enthusiastic alumni and those devoted professors who long to see him President of the United States have little hope of tempting him from his duties to his alma mater. Having set his hand to the plough, he must see Pluribus through her harvest season, and may God prosper the work! So, beloved of all, alumni and instructors alike, the idol of the undergraduates, a national oracle of Prosperity and Peace, President Butcher passes to a green old age, a truly Olympian figure of the time.

Impressions of Europe

1913–1914

Report to the Trustees of Columbia University

I T W A S M Y G O O D F O R T U N E as holder of the Gilder Fellowship in this University to spend in Europe the thirteen months immediately preceding the war. I used the opportunity for extensive travel and general acclimatization rather than for specialized research, and was thus able to get an extensive survey of the European scheme on the eve of a cataclysm from which it may emerge entirely altered. No one can predict how truly that year will mark the "end of an era." It seems true, however, that most of the tendencies of democracy, social reform, and international understanding, to whose development I gave my most eager attention, have been snapped off like threads, perhaps never to be pieced together again. And the material development, so striking in Germany and Italy, the rebuilding of the cities and the undertaking of vast communal projects, will be indefinitely checked, from sheer want of capital, wasted in the war.

No one was more innocent than I of the impending horror. In fact, this menacing "armed camp" actually seemed to bristle in less sharply defined lines when seen at close range. Public opinion seemed far less violent than I had expected. In England there was the persistent hostility to Compulsory Service, the gnawing compunction at the folly of the Boer War, the complete subsidence of the panic over German invasion. In France, there was the unyielding opposition to the new three-years' military law, culminating in the radical victory at the April parliamentary elections, a clear national expression of reluctance at the increased military expenditures; there was the superb irony of the French press over the Zabern affair, where one would have expected a raging chauvinism; there was the general public deprecation of the activities of the royalists, and the constant discrediting of their Alsace-Lorraine propaganda. In Italy I had seen the wild outburst of reaction against the criminal Tripolitan war, and the great general strike of June, a direct popular uprising against war and militarism. Perhaps if I had spent the winter in Germany, I should have felt the drift towards war, but even there all the opinion I heard was of some gigantic slow-moving Slavic pressure, against which defence must be made. And if public and press were full of blatant world-defiance, the spirit certainly escaped my attention. My mind became quite reconciled to the fact of "armed peace." My imagination unconsciously began to envisage armaments as mere frozen symbols of power, grim, menacing and costly, yet little more than graphic expressions, in a language that all the world could understand, of the relative strength and prestige of the nations. In spite of the uniforms that sprinkled the sidewalks and the wagon-trains that littered the streets, my imagination simply refused to take them as dynamic. And there was little in press and people to make me think that they themselves took them as dynamic. How I should have acted if I had known of the imminence of the world-war I do not know, but in the light of the event my rambles and interests take on the aspect of the toddlings of an innocent child about the edge of a volcano's crater.

I can give, however, a few indications of what such an innocent mind might see and feel in Europe, this year of last breathless hush before the explosion. I concerned myself with getting, first, a clear impression of the physical body in which each country clothed itself,—the aspect of town and countryside, villages, farms, working-class quarters, factories, suburbs, plans of towns, styles of architecture, characteristic types and ways of living, of modern Europe; and, second, the attitudes, social and political, of various classes, the social psychology of the different peoples. Such acquisitions had, of course, to be the merest impressions. One could not get "data"; one's tour could be little more than a perceptual "sizing-up." The best one could do was to settle down in the various capitals for a few months, immerse oneself in the newspapers, talk with as many people as one could reach, read the contemporary novels and plays, attend political meetings and meetings of social reformers, go to church and court-house and school and library and university, and watch the national life in action. One could only cut one-self off from American interests, imagine that one had always lived in the foreign city, and try, by a reach of sympathy and appreciation, to assimilate the tone and spirit and attitudes of the people among whom one was living. Such an effort may result only in the most fantastic illusions. I am not trying to boast that I got any understanding of European countries,—a matter of years of acquaintance and not of months. I am merely indicating an attitude of approach. But it was an attitude I found none too common among American students abroad. Among the many who were conducting historical and political researches at the libraries, I was never able to find any student interested in the political meetings of the campaign, for instance, which I attended with so much ardor, as a revelation of French social psychology. The Americans I saw would have an enthusiasm for particular things, perhaps, that they were interested in, a patronizing attitude towards certain immoralities and inefficiencies that impressed them, but as for a curiosity about the French mind and the French culture as a whole, I could not find any interest that flowed along with mine. My curiosity, therefore, had to go its own gait. I seemed to have a singular faculty for not getting information. Unless one is fortunate enough to step into a social group, one must dig one's way along unaided. By means of newspapers and magazines and guide-books, one hews out a little passage towards the center of things. Slowly a definite picture is built up of the culture and psychology of the people among whom one is living. There is no way, however, of checking up one's impressions. One must rely on one's intuition. Letters of introduction bring out only class or professional attitudes. Very few people are socially introspective enough to map out for you the mind of the society in which they live. Only the French seem to have this self-consciousness of their own traits, and the gift of expression, and that is why France is incomparably the most interesting and enlightening country for the amateur and curious American student to visit.

These considerations suggest the fact that I wish to bring out,—that my most striking impression was the extraordinary toughness and homogeneity of the cultural fabric in the different countries, England, France, Italy and Germany, that I studied. Each country was a distinct unit, the parts of which hung together, and interpreted each other, styles and attitudes, literature, architecture, and social organization. This idea is of course a truism, yet brought up, as most Americans are, I think, with the idea that foreigners are just human beings living on other parts of the earth's surface, "folks" like ourselves with accidental differences of language and customs, I was genuinely shocked to find distinct national temperaments, distinct psychologies and attitudes, distinct languages that embodied, not different sounds for the same meanings, but actually different meanings. We really know all this; but when we write about the war, for instance, we insensibly fall back to our old attitude. Most American comment on the war, even the most intelligent, suggests a complete ignorance of the fact that there is a German mind, and a French mind and an English mind, each a whole bundle of attitudes and interpretations that harmonize and support each other. And each of these national minds feels its own reasons and emotions and justifications to be cosmically grounded, just as we ourselves feel that Anglo-Saxon morality is Morality, and Anglo-Saxon freedom Liberty. We do, of course, more or less dimly recognize these differences of national culture. We no longer think of other nations as "Barbarians," unless they have a national scheme which is as much of a challenge to our own social inefficiency as is the German. We express our sense of the difference by a constant belittling. Foreigners are not monsters, but Lilliputians, dwarfs, playing with toys. We do not take other cultures seriously. We tend to dwell on the amusing, the quaint, the picturesque, rather than the intense emotional and intellectual differences. The opportunity to immerse oneself in these various cultures until one feels their powerful and homogeneous strength, their meaning and depth, until one takes each with entire seriousness and judges it, not in American terms, but in its own,—this is the educative value of a rapid, superficial European year such as mine. The only American book I have ever been able to find that deals with a foreign country in this adequate sense is Mr. Brownell's "French Traits." Almost all other writing, political, historical, descriptive, about European countries, must be read with the constant realization that the peculiar emotional and intellectual biases of the people, the temperamental traits, the soul which animates all their activities and expressions, have all been omitted from consideration by the author.

I can only give fragmentary hints in this short article of the incidents which built up my sense of these differences of national cultures. London was the place where I had the best opportunities for meeting people through letters of introduction. There were glimpses of the Webbs at a meeting of the Fabian Society, which seems to retain the allegiance of its old members rather than enlist the enthusiasm of the younger generation. At their house Mr. Webb talked, as he lectures, with the patient air of a man expounding arithmetic to backward children, and Mrs. Webb, passive by his side, spoke only to correct some slight slip on his part; there was another picture of her sweeping into the *New Statesman* office and producing a sudden panic of reverent awe among the editorial staff. Lectures by Shaw and Chesterton on succeeding nights—Shaw, clean, straight, clear and fine as an upland wind and summer sun; Chesterton, gluttonous and thick, with something tricky and unsavory about him—gave me a personal estimate of their contrasted philosophies. Then there was Professor Hobhouse, excessively judicial, with that high consciousness of excellence which the Liberal professor seems to exude; Graham Wallas, with his personal vivacity of expression and lack of any clear philosophy, who considered the American sociologist a national disaster; H. G. Wells, a suggestive talker, but very disappointing personally; John A. Hobson, whom I cannot admire too much, a publicist with immense stores of knowledge, poise of mind, and yet radical philosophy and gifts of journalistic expression, a type that we simply do not seem to be able to produce in this country.

I expected to find the atmosphere of London very depressing. On the contrary, a sort of fatuous cheerfulness seemed to reign everywhere on the streets, in middle-class homes, even in the slums. This impressed me as the prevailing tone of English life. Wells and Bennett seem to have caught it exactly. As for the world that Mr. Galsworthy lives in, though I looked hard for his people, I could find nothing with the remotest resemblance. Such a tone of optimism is possible only to an unimaginative people who are well schooled against personal reactions, and against the depressing influences of environment—slums and fog and a prevailing stodginess of middle-class life—that would affect the moods of more impressionable peoples. In certain educated circles this tone gave an impression of incorrigible intellectual frivolity. London has fashions in talk. Significant discussion almost did not exist. A running fire of ideational badinage, "good talk," took its place. Every idea tended to go up in smoke. You found your tone either monstrously prophetic, as of a young Jeremiah sitting at the board, or else unpleasantly cynical. Irony does not seem to be known in England.

The impression one got from the newspapers and magazines and popular books was of a sort of exuberant irrelevance, a vivacity of interest about matters that seemed

82

quite alien to the personal and social issues of life as one knew it. There seemed indeed to be a direct avoidance of these issues. One could never discover whether or how much an Englishman "cared." The national mind seemed to have made a sort of permanent derangement of intellect from emotion. In no country is so large a proportion of the literary product a mere hobby of leisurely gentlemen whose interests are quite elsewhere. The literary supplements of the newspapers used to contain the greatest collection of futilities that I ever saw. One got the impression that the intellectual life of the country was "hobbyized," that ideas were taken as sports, just as sports were taken as serious issues. This impression was rather confirmed at Oxford, where the anthropologist, Marrett, turned out to be a Jersey country gentleman, digging up prehistoric bones on his place, and mentioning Chesterton as "entertaining writer—even had him down here to lunch, but not a 'gentleman,' you know, not a 'gentleman.'" Oxford itself seemed to be one long play of schoolboys in the soft damp November air. Schiller, who gave me a delightful morning, after I had attended his class where the boys came in their black gowns and sat at primitive desks in the low room before a blazing fire, from which one looked out on mouldering walls and dead ivy and the pale morning sun and wan sweet decay, drew a wicked picture of the dons satisfying their thwarted sporting instincts by putting their boys through their intellectual paces and pitting them against each other in scholastic competition like race-horses. Mr. Mc-

Dougall, large and with an Irish courtliness, I heard and liked, and Mr. L. P. Jacks talked with me at Manchester College. A meeting of the Fabians at St· John's and a lecture by Mrs. Pember Reeves on "Coöperation" attracted me, with her dramatic flaring out at the stolid audience for their "English" lack of imagination—she came from New Zealand—the inanely facetious comments of the dons, the lumbering discourses of certain beefy burgesses from the local "Coöperative," who had not followed well the lady's nimble thought. Every little incident of the Oxford week of classes and rambles fitted into a picture of the place as a perfect epitome of English life, past and present. It was even more than London a world.

Politically, London was dead that autumn. No parliament, and every one weary of politics. The bitter Dublin strike dragged along with its reverberations through the English labor situation, which showed unrest and dissatisfaction with its leaders and much more of "syndicalist" leaning than any one would admit. A debate, heard later in Paris, hit the English labor situation off beautifully,— Longuet, arguing that there was no syndicalism in England because all the leaders had written him there wasn't; Joyaux, arguing that there was, because the unions were using forms of "direct actions" and acting exactly "as if" syndicalist ideas were spreading.

The Lloyd George land campaign for the bettering of rural labor conditions was begining, but was arousing so little enthusiasm that, with the intense dissatisfaction over the Insurance Acts that rose from every class, one wondered if the energy of the Liberal social program had about spent itself. The London press, solidly Tory—extraordinary situation for a Liberal country—was finding, besides its social grievances, the Ulster theme to play upon. Indefatigable industry, worthy of a better cause, was apparently being exercised to drum up reluctant English sentiment against Home Rule. All that autumn we lived ostensibly on the brink of a civil war, whose first mutterings did not even occur till the next July.

The suffragettes were quiescent, but their big meetings at Knightsbridge gave one a new insight into the psychology of the movement. As one watched this fusion of the grotesque and the tragic, these pale martyrs carried in amidst the reverent hush of a throng as mystically religious as ever stood around the death-bed of a saint; or as one heard the terrific roars of "Shame!" that went up at the mention of wrongs done to women, one realized that one was in the presence of English emotion, long starved and dried from its proper channels of expression, and now breaking out irrepressibly into these new and wild ways. It was the reverse side of the idolized English "reticence." It was a pleasant little commentary on the Victorian era. Suffragettism is what you get when you turn your whole national psychic energy into divorcing emotion from expression and from intellect.

A hysterical Larkin meeting in Albert Hall; meetings of the Lansbury people in the East End, with swarms of capped, cheerful, dirty, stodgy British workmen; a big Churchill meeting at Alexandra Palace, from which seventeen hecklers were thrown out, dully, one after the other, on their heads, after terrific scrimmages in the audience; quieter lectures at the Sociological Society, etc.; churches and law-courts, and tutorial classes, and settlements, and garden cities, and talks with many undistinguished people, rounded out my London impression, and in December I moved my stage to Paris.

The weeks of getting a hearing acquaintance with the language were spent in reading sociology at the Bibliothèque Ste. Geneviève, exchanging conversation with students at the Sorbonne, and attending still not understood lectures, in the hope that some day the electric spark of apprehension might flash. I soon felt an intellectual vivacity, a sincerity and candor, a tendency to think emotions and feel ideas, that integrated again the spiritual world as I knew it, and wiped out those irrelevances and facetiousnesses and puzzle-interests and sporting attitudes towards life, that so got on one's nerves in England. Here was also a democracy, not a society all shot into intellectual and social castes, where one lived shut in with ideas and attitudes that, like the proverbial ostrich, annihilated the rest of the world. In England, unless you were a "social reformer," you did not know anything about anybody but your own class; in France there seemed to be scarcely any social reformers, but everybody assumed an intelligent interest in everything. In short, a democracy, where you criticized everything and everybody, and neither attempted to "lift" the "lower orders" nor "ordered yourself lowly and reverently towards your betters." There was a solid, robust air of equality, which one felt in no other country, certainly not our own. The labor movement had an air of helping itself, and its leaders showed an intellectuality that ranked them with the professional men. In fact, the distinction between the "intellectual" and the non-intellectual seems to have quite broken down in France. Manners, styles of speech, pronunciation, ideas, the terms in which things are phrased, seem to flow rather freely over all the classes. Class-distinctions, which hit you in the face in England and America—I mean, differences of manner and speech, attitudes of contempt or admiration for other types—are much blurred. The language has remained simple, pure, usable without the triteness and vulgarity which dogs English, and which constitutes the most subtle evidence of our inherent Anglo-Saxon snobbery. It was a new world, where the values and the issues of life got reinstated for me into something of their proper relative emphasis.

With few letters of introduction, acclimatization was much more difficult than in London. One had to hew one's way around by the aid of the newspapers. These are infinitely more expressive of every shade of political opinion than is the London press. They provided a complete education in the contemporary world. Supplemented by the interesting symposiums in the reviews, and the mapping-out of the various French intellectual worlds which the young *agrégés* and instructors I met were always eager to give me, the Paris press provided a witty, interpretative daily articulation of the French mind at work. It is a very self-conscious and articulate mind, interested in the psychological artistic aspects of life rather than the objective active aspects which appeal to the English. Life to the Anglo-Saxon is what people are doing; to the Latin, rather the stream of consciousness, what individuals and also what groups are thinking and feeling. This all makes for clear thinking, constant interpretation —I noticed that my young lawyer friend was all the time saying "Violà! mon explication!"—and an amount of what might be called social introspection that makes France the easiest as well as the most stimulating country to become acquainted with. The French are right in telling you that their scholarship is not the collection of insignificant facts, but the interpretation of significant ones, the only kind of scholarship that is worth anything.

In Paris, I continued my general policy of running down the various social institutions, churches, courts, schools, political meetings, model tenements, etc., in order to get, at least, a taste of French society in operation. I poked about the various quarters of town and countryside, and talked to as many people as I could meet. After the lectures at the Sorbonne became intelligible, I followed the public courses of Bouglé and Delacroix and Durkheim in sociology, and when the campaign for the parliamentary election came I plunged into that, following the bulletin boards of the parties, with their flaring manifestoes—among them the royalists' "A Bas La République!" calmly left posted on the government's own official bulletin-board, as evidence of the most superb political tolerance I suppose any country has ever shown! —and attending the disorderly meetings held in the dingy playrooms of the public schoolhouses or in crowded cafés. French freedom of speech has been struggled for too long not to be prized when won, and the refusal to silence interrupters made each meeting a contest of wits and eloquence between the speaker and his audience. The most extraordinary incident of "fair play" I ever saw— Anglo-Saxons simply do not know what "fair play" is— was at one of Bouglé's meetings, where the chairman allowed one of his political opponents, who had repeatedly interrupted Bouglé, to take the platform and hold it for half an hour, attacking Bouglé and stating his own creed. When he had finished Bouglé took him up point by point, demolished him, and went on with his own exposition. This at his own meeting, called by his own Radical Party, to forward his candidature! When I left at 12:45 A.M. the meeting was still in progress. At a Socialist meeting an old Catholic, looking exactly like Napoleon III, was allowed to hold forth for several minutes from a chair, until the impatient audience howled him off. Young *normaliennes*, representing the suffrage movement, appeared at meetings of all the parties, and were given the platform to plead the cause of women as long as the crowd would listen. These young girls were treated exactly as men; there was no trace of either chivalry or vulgarity; the audience reacted directly and intensely to their ideas and not to them. The first impulse of a Frenchman actually seems to be, when he hears something he doesn't like, not to stop the other fellow's mouth, but to answer him, and not with a taunt, or disarming wit, but with an argument. In the Chamber of Deputies the same spirit prevailed. The only visible signs of parliamentary order were Deschanel's clashing of his big bell and his despairing "Voulez-vous écouter! Voulez-vous écouter!" The speaker in the tribune held it as long as he was permitted by his hearers; his interrupter would himself be interrupted and would exchange words across the chamber while the official speaker looked resignedly on. The Left would go off as one man in violent explosions of wrath, shake their fists at the Center, call out epithets. Yet this was a dull session that I saw, only a matter of raising the pay of generals. Certainly the campaign of that election against the new Three Years' Military Law seems very far away now. The crowd outside the Mairie of the Vme the night of the election shouting "A—Bas—Les-Trois-Ans," in the same rhythmic way that the law-students a few weeks earlier had marched down rue St. Jacques yelling "Cail—laux—as-sas-sin!" knew no more than I how soon they would need this defence of more soldiers. The cheers of the crowd as the splendid cortege of the English sovereigns swept along the streets seem more important than they did to me at the time. Doumergue's stand-pat ministry, with which my stay in Paris almost exactly coincided, and during which the income-tax, lay-instruction, and proportional representation issues slowly made progress, appears now in the light of a holding everything safe till the election was over, and the President could stem the tide of reaction against the new military laws. France was waiting for the blow to fall that might be mortal.

On the first of May I was in Nîmes, delightful Southern city,—where gaunt Protestants gave out tracts in the cars, and newspapers devoted to bull-fighting graced the news-stands,—reading the big red posters of the socialist mayor, summoning all the workmen to leave off work and come out to celebrate the International. Indeed a foreign land!

I arrived in Genoa the evening the Kaiser landed from Corfu, and witnessed the pompous and important event. In Pisa, I stepped into a demonstration of students, who were moving rapidly about the city closing the schools and making speeches to each other, as a protest against harsh treatment of Italians by the Austrian government in Trieste, the passionate *leit motiv* of Italia Irredenta that runs through all current Italian thought and feeling. In Florence I began to understand "futurism," that crude and glaring artistic expression which arises from the intolerable ennui of the ancient art with which the young Italian is surrounded, the swarms of uncritical foreigners, the dead museums. That Mona Lisa smile of Florence drove me soon to Rome, where I sensed the real Italy, with its industrial and intellectual ferment, its new renaissance of the twentieth century.

Rome is not a city, it is a world. Every century, from the first to the twentieth, has left its traces. It is the one city in Europe to study western civilization, an endless source of suggestion, stimulation and delight. It is the one city where the ancient and the ultra-modern live side by side, both brimming over with vitality. The Church and the most advanced and determined body of social revolutionists living side by side; the Vatican galleries faced by the futurist; a statue of Ferrer just outside Bernini's colonnade; rampant democracy confronting Prince Colonnas and Borgheses; Renaissance palaces, and blocks of monstrous apartments built in the mad speculation after 1870; all the tendencies and ideas of all Europe contending there in Rome, at once the most ancient and the most modern city we know. What is a month in Rome!

I could do little more than disentangle the political currents, get familiar with certain names in the intellectual world, and plot out the city, historically and sociologically, after a fashion. A noted psychologist, Dr. Assagioli in Florence, had gone over the philosophical situation for me; and in Rome, Professor Pettazoni of the university told me of the political tendencies. A young Modernist priest, discharged from his theological professorship for suspected connection with the "Programma," who talked about as much English as I did Italian, proved very friendly and informing, and gave me a sense of that vast subterranean, resistless, democratizing and liberalizing movement in the Church. Various types, Italian cavalry officers, professors of pedagogy, Sicilian lawyers, an emotional law student from Lecce, who took me to the university and talked republicanism to me, passed through the pension. And in Rome anyway you simply seeped Italy in, from the newspapers, as vivid and varied as those in Paris, and the host of little democratic and political weeklies, most of them recent, but fervent and packed with ideas that indicated a great ferment of young intellectual Italy. The young Florentine Papini gives in his picturesque books the picture of the Italian soul struggling with French, English and German ideas, and trying to hew some sort of order out of the chaos. One got the impression that Nietzsche was raging through the young Italian mind. But I was all for the candor and sympathy and personality of this expression. Papers like "La Voce," published by Papini's friends, have an idealistic sweep such as we simply cannot imagine or, I suppose, appreciate in this country. I had touched a different national mind. Expressions which seem wild to us fell there into their proper and interpretative order.

My impression was that almost anything might happen in Italy. While I was in Rome, the Pope was drawing protests from even the most conservative clerical dailies for his obscurantism. The country seemed to be disillusionizing itself about representative government, which, though it had become perfectly democratic, and had the most sweeping program of social reform, was clumsy and ineffective, and had utterly failed to carry out the popular hopes. The Crown scarcely seemed to be taken much more seriously than in Norway. Republican sentiment cropped up in unexpected places. Nationalism grew

apace, cleverly stimulated by the new capitalistic bourgeoisie and the new industry, which first impressed you
as you came through the long string of gayly-colored,
swarming factory towns on the coast between Ventimig-
lia and Genoa. Political parties, Nationalist, Constitution-
alist, Republican, Socialist, etc., seemed as numerous as in
France, but there was not the same fluctuation, for the
expert governmental hand kept a majority, in the Camera.
This body gave little of the impression of dignity that one
had felt in the French Chamber. One felt that while in
Italy democratic feeling was almost as genuine and universal as in France, political democracy had by no means
proved its worth. That Latin passion for intellectual sincerity and articulation—that quality which makes the
Latin the most sympathetic and at the same time the most
satisfactory person in the world, because you can always
know that his outward expression bears some relation to
his inward feeling—had resulted, as in France, in the du-
plication of parties, which were constantly holding con-
gresses and issuing programs, and then splitting up into
dissentient groups. This trait may be unfortunate politically; but it certainly makes for sincerity and intelligence, and all the other virtues which our Anglo-Saxon
two-party system is well devised to destroy.

This Latin quality of not being reticent, of reacting
directly and truthfully, had its most dramatic expression
in the great general strike of June, which I witnessed in
Rome. Disgust and chagrin at the Tripolitan war, a general reaction against militarism, had been slowly accumu-

lating in the working classes, and the smouldering feeling was touched off into a revolutionary explosion by the shooting of two demonstrators at Ancona by the police on the festival day of the Statuto. This was followed in Rome, as in most of the other cities of Italy, by a complete suspension of work. No cars or wagons moved for three days; no shops or stores opened their doors; none of the public services were performed; the only newspaper was a little red "bolletino" which told of the riots of the day before. One did nothing but walk the garbage-littered streets, past the shuttered windows and barricaded doors, and watch the long lines of infantry surrounding the public squares, and the mounted carabinieri holding the Piazza del Popolo, to prevent meetings and demonstrations. The calm spirit of the troops, surrounded by the excited crowds, was admirable. And the overwhelming expression of social solidarity displayed by this suspended city made one realize that here were radical classes that had the courage of their convictions. On the third day, the conservative classes recovered their breath, and I saw the slightly fearful demonstration of shouting youths who moved down the Via del Tritone while great Italian flags swung out from one window after another, greeted with wild hand-clapping from every thronged bourgeois balcony. The next day the darting trolley-cars told the strike was over, but two days later I alighted at the Naples station into a fortress held by Bersaglieri against a mob who had been trying all day to burn the station. The shooting kept us inside until the last rioters were dispersed, and the great protest was over, though it was days before the people of the Romagna, where railroads and telegraphs were cut, were convinced that the monarchy had not fallen and a republic been proclaimed. The government had kept very quiet, except for the floods of oratory that rolled through the Camera; if it had not, there might have been a real revolution, instead of merely the taste and thrill of one.

My last political experience in Italy was election night in Venice, with the triumph of the conservatives, who had made no bones of the economic interpretation of politics, but had placarded the city with posters recalling to gondolieri, hotel-keepers and shop-keepers, the exact amount of money they had lost by reason of the general strike and the wild scurry of foreigners out of the country. This rather appalling sum was apparently a final and clinching argument, and we heard the gratitude of the Patriarch from his balcony by San Marco expressed to the citizens who had "saved" their country. Such incidents are symbols of the candors and delights of the Latin temperament and of everything in the Latin countries.

Switzerland, besides its holidaying, contributed the Bern Exposition, the intensely significant spectacle of a nation looking at itself. If, as was said, every Swiss school-child saw the exposition not once but three times, our day was one of those times. All Switzerland was there studying and enjoying itself. In this little epitome of its life, one had a sense of the refreshing value of living in a small country where its activities and spirit could all, in some sort of fashion, be grasped, understood, contemplated, as one might a large picture. Most suggestive, perhaps, were the great water-power development projects, electrical engineering schemes, and mountain railroading, planned ahead in a broad way for fifty years or so. A country that knew what it was about, that knew how to use its resources for large social ends!

My German tour of the last two weeks of July, cut short by the war, was more definitely sociological. I had been through the Rhine country to Heidelberg, Stuttgart, and Munich, the preceding summer. This trip went straight north from Friedrichshaften to Berlin. There were the famous town-planned cities to be seen, and housing-schemes, which I had followed rather closely in all the countries, and a general "sizing-up" of German "Kultur." I missed my settling down in Berlin; newspapers and people had to be taken on the wing. But then the German spirit and expression was much more familiar to me through study than had been the French and Italian. My most striking impression was of the splendor of the artistic renaissance, as shown particularly in the new architecture and household and decorative and civic art. These new and opulent styles are gradually submerging that fearful debauch of bad taste which followed the French war, and which makes the business quarters of the German cities so hideous. But the newer quarters, monuments, public buildings of the last ten years have a massive, daring style which marks an epoch in art. I have yet to come across an American who likes this most recent German architecture; but to me buildings like the University at Jena, the Stuttgart theater, the Tietz shops, etc., whith their heavy concrete masses and soaring lines, speak of perfectly new and indigenous ideas. And if artistic creation is a mark of a nation's vitality, the significance of this fine flare and splurge of German style, the endless fecundity of decorative design in printing and furniture, etc.; the application of design to the laying out of towns and suburbs, the careful homogeneity and integrity of artistic idea, should not be overlooked. These things are fertile, are exhilarating and make for the enhancement of life. The Germans are acting exactly as if they no longer believed, as we do, that a high quality of urban life can be developed in a ragtag chaos of undistinguished styles and general planlessness.

Specifically, I visited the municipal workingmen's cottages in Ulm and saw the town-planning charts of the city in the office of the *Stadtbaurat;* the huge apartments, municipally built and owned, in Munich; the big *Volksbad* in Nuremberg, and the garden-city workingmen's suburb at Lichtenhof, with the schoolchildren's garden allotments; the model garbage-disposal plant at Furth, a miarcle of scientific resource and economy; the extraordinary model municipal slaughter-house at Dresden, so characteristically German with its *Schlachthof* and *Direktorhaus* at the entrance; and, lastly the famous garden-city of Hellerau, inferior, however, on the whole, to the English Hampstead Suburb at Golders Green. Towns like Rothenburg and Nordlingen were little laboratories of mediæval and modern town-planning. The *Stadt-baurat* at Rothenburg went over for us the development of the city, and gave us considerable insight into the government, policy and spirit of a typical little German municipality. Undemocratic in political form, yet ultra-democratic in policy and spirit, scientific, impartial, giving the populace—who seemed to have no sense of being excluded from "rights"—what they really wanted, far more truly than our democracies seem to be able to secure, this epitome of the German political scheme served to convince us that we were in a world where our ordinary neat categories of political thought simply didn't apply. It was futile to attempt an interpretation in Anglo-Saxon terms. There was no objective evidence of the German groaning under "autocracy" and "paternalism." One found oneself for the first time in the presence of a government between whom and the people there seemed to exist some profound and subtle sympathy, a harmony of spirit and ends.

It was dramatic to sweep up through the endless billowing fields and carefully tended forests and imposing factory towns—Germany, caught at mid-summer, in the full tide of prosperity—and come into Berlin on the morning of "the historic day," July 31st, 1914, with the agitated capital on the brink of war; to see the arrival of the Kaiser and the princes at the Schloss; to watch the Crown Prince's automobile blocked twenty feet away form us by the cheering crowd;—"der *wahre* Kriegesmann," as the papers were calling him in contemptuous contrast to his peaceful father; to hear the speech of the latter—grim, staccato-voiced, helmeted figure, very symbol of war—from the balcony of the palace; to watch next day the endless files of reservists marching through the streets to the casernes to "einkleiden"; and then to hear the finally fatal news of Russia's refusal with the swarming crowds on Unter den Linden, hysterical from both fervor and anxiety. If ever there was a tense and tragic moment, when destiny seemed concentrated into a few seconds of time, it was that 5 P.M. on the afternoon of August first, at the corner of Unter den Linden and Friedrichstrasse, in Berlin.

A midnight flight to Sweden, with a motley horde of scared Russians and Scandinavians, and two weeks in the distressed and anxious northern countries ended my year. Nothing but the war; regiments of flaxen-haired Danish boys, mobilizing along the country roads of Denmark, the *Landsturm* lolling along the Stockholm streets, even the Norwegians drilling against none knew what possible attack. The heavens had fallen. An interview with Herr Branting, the Swedish Socialist leader, and the depths of his personal feeling and the moving eloquence with which he went over the wreck of socialist and humanitarian hopes, gave us the vividest sense of the reverberations of the shock on a distinguished cosmopolitan mind. The librarian of the Royal Library in Copenhagen, the pastor of the Swedish church, and the editor of "Dagens Nyheter," in Stockholm, whom we were able to talk with, very kindly answered our questions on Scandinavian affairs. And we have the pleasantest memories of Herr Hambro in Christiania, editor of the leading Conservative daily, who had just finished La Follette's autobiography, and would have preferred to talk about America even to showing us how the Radical parties in Norway were lording it over their opponents. One got the sense in these countries of the most advanced civilization, yet without sophistication, a luminous modern intelligence that selected and controlled and did not allow itself to be overwhelmed by the chaos of twentieth-century possibility. There was a mood of both gravity and charm about the quality of the life lived, something rather more Latin than Teutonic. This is an intuition, reinforced by a sense that nowhere had I seen so many appealing people as on the streets of Copenhagen. Valid or not, it was the pleasantest of intuitions with which to close my year.

This sketch, I find, has, in fact, turned out much more impressionistic than I intended. But impressions are not meant to be taken as dogmas. I saw nothing that thousands of Americans have not seen; I cannot claim to have brought back any original contribution. There was only the sense of intimate acquaintance to be gained, that feeling of at-homeness which makes intelligible the world. To the University which made possible the rare opportunity of acquaintance with these various countries and cultures, the contact with which has been so incompletely suggested in this sketch, my immeasurable thanks!

Ernest:

or Parent for a Day

I HAD BEEN TALKING rather loosely about the bringing-up of children. They had been lately appearing to me in the guise of infinitely prevalent little beings who impressed themselves almost too vividly upon one's consciousness. My summer vacation I had passed in a household where a vivacious little boy of two years and a solemn little boy of six months had turned their mother into a household slave. I had seen walks, conversations, luncheons, and all the amenities of summer civilized life, shot to pieces by the indomitable need of imperious little children to be taken care of. Little boys who came running at you smiling, stubbed their toes, and were instantly transformed into wailing inconsolables; babies who woke importunately at ten o'clock in the evening, and had to be brought down warm and blinking before the fire; human beings who were not self-regulating, but to whom every hard surface, every protuberance, was a menace to happiness, and in whom every want and sensation was an order and claim upon somebody else—these were new offerings to my smooth and independent existence. They interested and perturbed me.

The older little boy, with his sunny luxuriance of hair and cheek, was always on the point of saying something novel and disconcerting. The baby, with his deep black eyes, seemed to be waiting silently and in soft anticipation for life. He would look at you so calmly and yet so eagerly, and give you a pleasant satisfaction that just your mere presence, your form, your movement, were etching new little lines on his cortex, sending new little shoots of feeling through his nerves. You were being part of his education just by letting his consciousness look at you. I liked particularly to hold my watch to his ear, and see the sudden grave concentration of his face, as he called all his mind to the judgment of this arresting phenomenon. I would love to accost him as he lay murmuring in his carriage, and to check his little breakings into tears by quick movements of my hands. He would watch me intently for a while until the fact of his little restless woe would come upon him again. I was challenged then to something more startling, and the woe would disappear in little short gasps. But I would find that he was subject to the law of diminishing returns. The moment would arrive when the woe submerged everything in a wail, and his mother would have to be called to nurse or coddle him in the magical motherly way.

The baby I found perhaps more interesting than his little brother, for the baby's moods had more style to them. The brother could be transformed from golden prattlingness to raging storm, with the most disconcerting quickness. He could want the most irrational things with an intensity that got itself expressed in hypnotic reiteration. Some smoldering will-to-power in one's self told one that a child should never be given the thing that he most wanted; and yet in five minutes one would have given him one's soul, to be rid of the brazen rod which he pounded through one. But I could not keep away from him. He and his baby brother absorbed me, and when I contemplated their mother's life, I had many a solemn sense of the arduousness of being a parent. I thought of the long years ahead of them, and the incalculability of their manifestations. I shuddered and remained, gloating, I am afraid, a little over the opportunity of enjoyment without responsibility.

All these things I was recounting the other evening after dinner to a group of friends who professionally look after the minds and bodies of the neglected. I was explaining my absorption, and the perils and merciless tyranny of the mother's life, and my thankfulness at having been so much in, and yet so much not of, the child-world. I was not responsible, and the policeman mother could be called in at any time to soothe or to quell. I could always maintain the amused aloofness which is my usual attitude toward children. And I made the point that parenthood must become less arduous after the child is a self-regulating little organism, and can be trusted not to commit suicide inadvertently over every threshold, can feed himself, dress himself, and take himself reasonably around. I even suggested unwarily that after five or six the tyranny was much mitigated.

There was strong dissent. Just at that age, I was told, the real responsibilities began. I was living in a fool's paradise of bachelordom if I thought that at six children were grown-up. One of the women before the fire made it her business to get children adopted. I had a sense of foreboding before she spoke. She promptly confirmed my intuition by offering to endow me with an infant of six years, for a day or for as long as I would take him. The hearty agreement of the rest amazed and alarmed me. They seemed delighted at the thought of my becoming parent for a day. I should have Ernest. They all knew Ernest; and I should have him. They seemed to have no concern that he would not survive my brief parenthood. It rather warmed and flattered me to think that they trusted me.

I had a sense of being caught in an inescapable net, prisoner of my own theories. If children of six were no longer tyrants, the possession of Ernest would not interfere with my work or my life. I had spoken confidently. I had a reputation among my friends of speaking eloquently about "the child." And I always find it almost impossible to resist the offer of new experience. I hesitated and was lost. I even found myself naming the day for Ernest's momentary adoption. And during all that week I found it increasingly impossible to forget him. The night before Ernest was to come I told myself that I could not believe that this perilous thing was about to happen to me. I made no preparations to receive Ernest in my tiny bachelor apartment. I felt that I was in the hands of fate.

II

I was not really surprised when fate knocked at the door next morning in the person of my grinning friend, and swiftly left a well-bundled little boy with me. I have rarely seen a young woman look as maliciously happy as did his guide when she left, with the remark that she couldn't possibly come for Ernest that evening, but would take him at nine o'clock on the morrow. My first quick resentment was stilled by the thought that perhaps an official day was a day plus a night. But Ernest loomed formidably at me. There would be problems of sleeping. Was I a victim? Well, that is what parents were! They should not find me weak.

Ernest expressed no aversion to staying with me. He was cheerful, a little embarrased, incurious. The removal of his hat disclosed a Dutch-cut of yellow hair, blue eyes, many little freckles, and an expression of slightly quizzical good-humor. I really had not had the least conception how big a boy of six was likely to be, and I found comfort in the evidence that he was big enough to be self-regulating, and yet deliciously small enough to be watched over. He could be played with, and without danger of breaking him.

Ernest sat passively on a chair and surveyed the room. I had thought a little pedantically of exposing him to some Montessori apparatus. I had got nothing, however. The room suddenly became very inane; the piano a huge packing-box, the bookcases offensive, idiotic shelves. A silly room to live in! A room practically useless for these new and major purposes of life. I was ashamed of my surroundings, for I felt that Ernest was surveying me with contempt and reproach.

It suddenly seemed as if little boys must like to look at pictures. Ernest had clambered up into a big chair, and was sitting flattened against its back, his legs sticking straight out in front of him, and a look of mild lassitude on his face. He took with some alacrity the illustrated newspaper supplement which I gave him, but my conscience tortured me a little as to whether his interest was the desperate one of demanding something for his mind to feed on, however arid it might be, or whether it was a genuine æsthetic response. He gave all the pictures exactly the same amount of time, rubbing his hand over each to make sure that it was flat, and he showed no desire to talk about anything he had seen. Since most of the pictures were of war, my pacifist spirit rebelled against dwelling on them. His celerity dismayed me. It became necessary to find more pictures. I had a sudden horror of an afternoon of picture-books, each devoured in increasingly accelerated fashion. How stupid seemed my rows of dully printed books! Not one of them could disgorge a picture no matter how hard you shook it. Despair seized me when I found only a German handbook of Greek sculpture, and another of Michelangelo. In hopeful trepidation I began on them. I wondered how long they would last.

It was clearly an unfamiliar field to Ernest. My attempts to test his classical knowledge were a failure. He recognized the Greeks as men and women, but not as gods, and there were moments when I was afraid he felt nudity as indecent. He insisted on calling the Winged Victory an angel. There had evidently been religion in Ernest's career. I told him that these were pictures of marble statues from Greece, of gods and things, and I hurriedly sketched such myths as I could remember in an attempt to overtake Ernest's headlong rush of interest. But he did not seem to listen, and he ended by calling every flowing female form an angel. He laughed greatly at their missing arms and heads. I do not think I quite impressed him with the Greek spirit.

On Michelangelo there was chance to test his Biblical background. He proved never to have heard of David, and took the story I told him with a little amused and incredulous chortle. Moses was new to him, and I could not make him feel the majesty of the horns and beard. When we came to the Sistine I felt the constraint of theology. Should I point out to him God and Adam and Eve, and so perhaps fix in his infant mind an ineradicable theological bias? Now I understand the temptation which every parent must suffer, to dose his child with easy mythology. Something urged me to say, Adam was the first man and

Eve was the first woman, and get the vague glow of having imparted godly information. But I am glad that I had the strength sternly to refrain, hoping that Ernest was too intellectually robust to be trifled with. I confined myself to pointing out the sweep of clouds, the majesty of the prophets, the cracks in the plaster, the mighty forms of the sibyls.

But with my last sibyl I was trapped. It smote my thought that there were no more pictures. And Ernest's passivity had changed. We were sitting on the floor, and his limbs began to take on movement. He crawled about, and I thought began to look menacingly at movable objects on tables. My phobia of the combination of movable objects and children returned. Parenthood suddenly seemed the most difficult thing in the world. Ernest was not talking very much, and I doubted my ability to hold him very long entranced in conversation. Imgaination came to my relief in the thought of a suburban errand. I remembered a wonderful day when I myself had been taken by my uncle to the next town on a journey—the long golden afternoon, the thundering expresses at the station, the amazing watch which he had unaccountably presented me with at the end of the day. Ernest should be taken to Brookfield.

Our lunch had to be taken at the railroad station. Ernest climbed with much puffing up to the high stool by the lunch-counter, and sat there unsteadily and triumphantly while I tried to think what little boys ate for their lunch. My decision for scrambled eggs and a glass of milk was unwise. The excitement of feeding scrambled eggs to a slippery little boy on top of a high stool was full of incredible thrills. The business of preventing a deluge of milk whenever Ernest touched his glass forced me to an intellectual concentration which quite made me forget my own eating. Ernest himself seemed in a state of measureless satisfaction; but the dizzy way in which he brandished his fork, the hairbreadth escape of those morsels of food as they passed over the abyss of his lap, the new and strange impression of smearedness one got from his face, kept me in a state of absorption until I found we had but one minute to catch our train. With Ernest clutching a large buttered roll which he had decently refused to relinquish, we rushed through the gates.

When the candy-man came through the train, Ernest asked me in the most detached tone in the world if I was going to buy any candy. And I asked him with a similar dryness what his preferences in candy were. He expressed a cool interest in lemon-drops. The marvelous way in which Ernest did not eat those lemon-drops gave me a new admiration for his self-control. He finished his buttered roll, gazed out of the window, casually ate two or three lemon-drops, and then carefully closed the box and put it in his pocket. I was almost jealous of Ernest's character. I recalled my incorrigible nibblings. I predicted for Ernest a moral life.

Our talk was mostly of the things that flashed past our eyes. I was interested in Ernest's intellectual background. Out of the waste of signboards and salt-meadows there was occasionally disentangled a river with boats or a factory or a lumber-yard which Ernest could be called upon to identify. He was in great good humor, squirming on his seat, and he took delight in naming things and in telling me of other trips on the railroad he had taken. He did not ask where we were going. I told him, but it seemed not especially to concern him. He was living in life's essential,—excitement,—and neither the future nor the past mattered. He held his own ticket a little incredulously, but without the sense of the importance of the business that I had looked for. I found it harder and harder not to treat him as an intellectual equal.

In Brookfield I became conscious of a desire to show Ernest off. I was acquiring a proprietary interest in him. I was getting proud of his good temper, his intelligence, his self-restraint, his capacity for enjoying himself. I wanted to see my pride reflected in another mind. I would take him to my wise old friend, Beulah. I knew how pleasurably mystified she would be at my sudden possession of a chubby, yellow-haired little boy of six.

Ernest had a delightful hour on Beulah's parlor floor. He turned somersaults, he shouted, he played that I was an evil monster who was trying to catch him. He would crawl up warily towards me and put his hand on my sleepily outstretched palm. As I suddenly woke and seized him, he would dart away in shrieks of fear and glee. When I caught him, I would feel like a grim ogre indeed, for his face would cloud and little tears shoot into his eyes, and his lips would curl in mortal fear. And then I would let him go tugging and sprawling, and he would yell with joy, and steal back with ever-renewed cunning and watchfulness. When he had eaten Beulah's cakes and drunk her cocoa, he lay back in a big chair, glowing with rosiness, and still laughing at the thought of his escape from my ogredom.

Our minds played about him. I tried to tease Beulah into adopting him. We spoke of his birth in a reformatory, and the apparently indomitable way in which nature had erased this fact from his personality. We wondered about his unknown mother, and his still more unknown father, and what he would be and how either of us could help keeping him forever. She pleaded her Man, I my poverty. But we were not convincing, and I began to conceive a vague fear of Ernest's adopting me, because I could not let him go.

And then it was time for the train. Ernest was very self-possessed. His manners on leaving Beulah were those of an equal, parting from a very old and jolly friend. The walk to the station gave me a sudden realization how very badly the world was adapted to the needs of little boys. Its measurements, its times, its lengths and its breadths were grotesquely exaggerated. Ernest ploughed manfully along, but I could feel the tug at my hand. Time would have to double itself for him to reach the station in the allotted minutes. His legs were going in great strides like those of the giant in seven-league boots, and he was panting a little. I was cruel, and yet there was the train. I felt myself a symbol of parenthood, earth-adjusted, fixed on an adult goal, dragging little children panting through a world not their own. "I'm ti-yerd!" said Ernest is so plaintive a voice that my heart smote me. Nameless premonitions of what might ensue to Ernest from being ti-yerd came upon me. I felt a vague dread of having already made Ernest an invalid for life. But my adulthood must have triumphed, for the train was caught. Ernest's spirits revived on the reappearance of the lemon-drops. And my heart leaped to hear him say that only his legs were ti-yerd, and that now they were no longer so. The world had diminished again to his size.

III

Ernest ate his supper in great contentment at a little table by my fireplace. The unaccustomed task of cooking it gave me new and vivid thrills. And the intellectual concentration involved in heating soup and making toast was so great as to lose me the pleasure of watching Ernest draw. I had asked him in the morning if he liked to draw. He had answered in such scorn that I had hastily called in Michelangelo. Now I placed a pencil and many large sheets of paper negligently near him. When I brought him his supper, he had covered them all with futuristic men, houses, and horses. The floor was strewn with his work, and he was magnificently casting it from him as he attacked these æsthetic problems with fierce gusto. Only the sight of food quelled his artistic rage. After supper, however, he did not return to them. Instead, he became fascinated with the pillows of my couch, and piled them in a line, with a whistling and shouting as of railroad trains. I wrote a little, merely to show myself that this business of parenthood need not devastate one's life. But I found myself wondering acutely, in the midst of an eloquent sentence, what time it was healthy for Ernest to go to bed. I seemed to remember seven—incredible to me, and yet perhaps meet for a child. It was already seven, but the vigor with which he rejected my proposal startled me. His amiability all day had been so irreproachable that I did not wish to strain it now. Yet I was conscious of an approaching parental crisis. Suppose he did not want to go to bed at all!

When I next looked up, I found that he had compromised by falling asleep in a curious diagonal and perilous position across his pillows—the trainman asleep at the switch. In a position in which nobody could sleep, Ernest slept with the face of an angel. Complexity! Only a brute would wake him. Yet how did parents get their children to bed? And then I thought of the intricacies of his clothes. I touched him very gently; he jumped at me in a dazed way, with the quaintest, "Oh, I don't know what made me go to sleep!" and was off into the big chair and helpless slumber.

I repented of my brutality. I tried to read, but my parental conscience again smote me. Ernest looked forlorn and maladjusted, his head sinking down on his breast. I thought that Ernest would thank me now for reminding him of his bed. He showed astonishing force of will. I recoiled from the "I don't want to go to bed!" which he hurled at me. I tried reason. I called his attention to his uncomfortableness. But he was unmoved, and insisted on going to sleep again after every question. I hardened my heart a little. I saw that stern measures would have to be adopted, Ernest's little clothes taken off, Ernest inserted into his flannel nightgown, and tucked into bed. Yet I had no idea of the parental technique for such situations. Ernest had been quite irresponsible to my appeal that all good little boys went to bed at seven o'clock, and I could think of no further generalizations. Crisis after so happy a day! Was this parenthood?

The variety of buttons and hooks on Ernest's outer and inner garments bewildered me. Ernest's dead sleepiness made the work difficult. But finally his little body emerged from the midst, leaving me with the feeling of one who has taken a watch apart and wonders dismayedly how he will ever get it together again. Ernest, however, was not inclined to permit the indignity of this disrobing without bitter protest. When I urged his coöperation in putting on his nightgown, he became voluble. The sunniness of his temper was clouded. His tone turned to harsh bitterness. Little angry tears rolled down his cheeks, and he betrayed his sense of extreme outrage with an "I don't *want* to put on my nightgown!" hurled at me with so much of moral pain that I was chilled. But it was too late. I could not unscramble Ernest. With a sinking heart I had gently to thrust his little arms and legs into the warm flannel, trundle him over the floor, bitter and sleepily protesting, roll him into his bed, and cover him up. As he curled and snuggled into the covers his tears dried as if by magic, the bitterness smoothed out of his face, and all his griefs were forgotten.

IV

In the next room I sat and read, a pleasant warmth of parental protection in my heart. And then Ernest began to cough. It was no light childish spasm, but a deep racking cough that froze my blood. There had been a little cold in him when he came. I had taken him out into the raw December air. I had overexerted him in my thoughtless haste. Visions of a delirious and pneumonic child floated before me. Or what was that dreadful thing called croup? I could not keep my thought on my book. That racking cough came again and again. Ernest must be awake and tossing feverishly. Yet when I looked in at him, he would be lying peaceful and rosy, and the cough that tore him did not disturb his slumbers. He must then be in a state of fatigue so extreme that even the cough could not wake him. I reproached myself for dragging him into the cold. How could I have led him on so long a journey, and let him play with a strenuousness such as his days never knew! I foresaw a lurid to-morrow: Ernest sick, myself helpless and ignorant, guilty of a negligence that might be fatal. And as I watched him, he began to show the most alarming tendency to fall out of bed. I did not dare to move him, and yet his head moved ever more perilously near the edge. I relied on a chair pushed close to the bed to save him. But I felt weary and worn. What an exacting life, the parent's! Could it be that every evening provided such anxieties and problems and thrills? Could one let one's life become so engrossed?

And then I remembered how every evening, when we went to bed, we used to ask our mother if she was going to be home that evening, and with what thankful security we sank back, knowing that we should be protected through another night. Ernest had not seemed to care what became of me. Having had no home and no parents, he had grown up into a manly robustness. He did not ask what you were going to do with him. He was all for the moment. He took the cash and let the credit go. It was I who felt the panic and the insecurity. I envied Ernest. I saw that contrary to popular mythology, there were advantages in being an institutional orphan, provided you had been properly Binet-ed as of normal intelligence and the State got you a decent boarding-mother. How much bringing up Ernest had escaped! If his manners were not polished, at least they were not uncouth. He had been a little shy at first, nodding at questions with a smile, and throwing his head against the chair. But there was nothing repressed about him, nothing institutional-ized, and certainly nothing artificial.

His cough grew lighter, and as I looked at his yellow hair and the angelic flush of his round cheeks, I thought of the horrid little puppets that had been produced around me in conventional homes, under model fathers and kind and devout mothers. How their fears and inhibitions contrasted with Ernest's directness! His bitter mood at going to bed had a certain fine quality about it. I recalled the *camaraderie* we had established. The box of lemon-drops, only half-exhausted, stared at me from the pocket of his little sweater. I became proud of Ernest. I was enjoying again my vicarious parenthood. What did that obscure and tangled heredity of his, or his most problematical of futures, matter to him or to me? It was delightful to adopt him thus imaginatively. If he turned out badly, could you not ascribe it to his heredity, and if well, to your kindly nurture and constant wisdom? Nothing else could be very much thought about, perhaps, but for the moment Ernest seemed supremely worth thinking about. There would be his education. And suddenly it seemed that I did not know very much about educating a child. It would be too absorbing. There would be no time for the making of a living. Ernest loomed before my imagination in the guise of a pleasant peril.

And then morning came. As soon as it was light Ernest could be heard talking and chuckling to himself, with no hint of delirium or pneumonia, or the bogies of the night. When I spoke he came running in in his bare feet, and crawled in with me. He told me that in spite of my valiant chair he had really fallen out of bed. He did not care, and proceeded to jump over me in a vigorous acrobatic way. He did not even cough, and I wondered if all the little sinister things of childhood passed so easily with the night. It was impossible to remember my fears as he tossed and shouted, the perfection of healthiness. Parenthood now seemed almost too easy to bother with.

Ernest caught sight of my dollar watch on the chair, and I saw that he conceived a fatal and instantaneous passion. He listened to its tick, shook it, ogled it amorously. He made little suggestive remarks about liking it. I teased him with the fact that he could not tell time. Ernest snorted at first in good-natured contempt at the artificial rigidity of the process, but finally allowed himself to be persuaded that I was not fooling him. And my heart swelled with the generosity which I was about to practise in presenting him with this wonderful watch.

But it suddenly became time to dress, for my parental day was to end at nine. And then I discovered that it was as hard to get Ernest into his clothes as it was to get him out of them. It was intolerable to him that he should leave his romp and the watch, and he shouted a No to my every suggestion. A new parental crisis crashed upon me. What a life of ingenuity and stratagem the parent had to lead! To spend half one's evening persuading a sleepy and bitter little boy to take off his clothes, and half the morning in persuading a vivid and jubilant little boy to put them on again—this was a life that taxed one's personal resources to the utmost. I reasoned with Ernest. I pointed out that his kind friend was coming very soon, and that he must be ready. But Ernest was obdurate. He would not even bathe. I pointed out the almost universal practice of the human race of clothing themselves during the early morning hours. Historic generalizations had no more effect on Ernest in the morning than they had had in the evening. And with a sudden stab I thought of the watch. That watch I knew would be an Aladdin's lamp to make Ernest my obedient slave. I had only to bribe him with it, and he would bathe, dress, or do anything which I told him to do. Here was the easy art of corruption by which parents got moral clutches on their children! And I deliberately renounced it. I would not bribe Ernest. Yet the mischief was done. So intuitive was his mind that I felt guiltily that he already knew my readiness to give him the watch if he would only dress. In that case, I should miss my moral victory. I could not disappoint him, and I did not want to bribe him inadvertently.

There was another consideration which dismayed me. Even if Ernest should prove amenable to reason or corruption, where was my ability to reconstruct him? Unbuttoning a sleepy and scarcely resisting little boy in the evening was quite different from constructively buttoning a jumping and hilarious one in the morning. And time was flowing dangerously on. Only a sudden theory of self-activity saved me. Could Ernest perhaps dress himself? I caught him in one of his tumbles and asked him. His mind was too full of excitement, to be working on prosaic themes. And then I shot my bolt. "I don't believe you know how to dress yourself, do you?" To that challenge Ernest rose. "Hurry!" I said, "and see how quickly you can dress. See if you can dress before I can!" Ernest flew into the other room, and in an incredibly short time appeared quite constructed except as to an occasional rear-button, washed and shining, self-reliant, ready for the business of the day. I glowed with the success of my parental generalship. I felt a sense of power. But power gained in so adroit and harmless a way was safe. What a parent I would make! How grateful I was to Ernest to be leaving me at this height!

I gave him the watch. Though he had longed, the fulfillment of his desire struck him with incredulity. The event awed him. But I showed him how to wind it, and seemed so indifferent to its fate that he was reassured as to my sincerity. He recovered his poise. He sang as he ate his breakfast. And when his guide and friend came, amused and curious, he went off with her as unreluctantly as he had come, proud and self-possessed, the master of himself. He strutted a little with his watch, and he politely admitted that he had had a good time.

I do not know whether Ernest ever thought of me again. He had been an unconscious artist, for he had painted many new impressions on my soul. He had been sent to me to test my theories of parenthood, but he had driven away all thought of theory in the obsession of his demands. How could I let him go cheerily out of my door? It wasn't at all because I minded having my time absorbed, for I like people to absorb my time. Why did I not cling to him, buy him from his protector, with a "Dear boy, you shall never leave my pleasant rooms again"? Why did I not rush after him down the street, stung by a belated remorse? I was conscious enough that I was missing all the dramatic climax of the situation. I was not acting at all as one does with tempting little orphan boys. But that is the way life works. The heart fails, and the vast and incalculable sea of responsibility drowns one in doubt. I let him go with no more real hesitation than that with which he went.

The later life of Ernest I feel will be one of sturdy self-reliance. That all the aspects of his many-sided character did not become apparent in the short time that I held him was clear from the report I heard of a Christmas party to which he was invited a few weeks later. Ernest, it seems, had broken loose with the fervor of a modern Europe after its forty years of peace. He had seized chocolate cake, slapped little girls, bitten the hand of the kind lady who fed him, and ended by lying down on the floor and yelling in a self-reliant rage. Was this the effect of a day with me? Or had I charmed and soothed him? I had a pleasant shudder of power, wondering at my influence over him.

The next I heard of Ernest was his departure for the home of an adopting family in New Jersey, from which he was presently to be shipped back for offenses unknown. My respect for Ernest rose even higher. He would not fit in easily to any smug conventional family life. He would not rest adopted until he was satisfied. I began to wonder if, after all, we were not affinities. He had kept the peace with me, he had derived stimulation from my society. Should I not have called him back? Shall I not now? Shall I not want to see him with me again? I wonder.

The Art of
Theodore Dreiser

THEODORE DREISER has had the good fortune to
evoke a peculiar quality of pugnacious interest among
the younger American intelligentsia such as has been the
lot of almost nobody else writing to-day unless it be Miss
Amy Lowell. We do not usually take literature seriously
enough to quarrel over it. Or else we take it so seriously
that we urbanely avoid squabbles. Certainly there are
none of the vendettas that rage in a culture like that of
France. But Mr. Dreiser seems to have made himself, particularly since the suppression of "The Genius," a veritable issue. Interesting and surprising are the reactions to
him. Edgar Lee Masters makes him a "soul-enrapt demi-
urge, walking the earth, stalking life"; Harris Merton
Lyon saw in him a "seer of inscrutable mien"; Arthur
Davison Ficke sees him as master of a passing throng of
figures, "labored with immortal illusion, the terrible and
beautiful, cruel and wonder-laden illusion of life"; Mr.
Powys makes him an epic philosopher of the "life-tide";
H. L. Mencken puts him ahead of Conrad, with "an ag-
nosticism that has almost passed beyond curiosity." On

the other hand, an unhappy critic in *The Nation* last year gave Mr. Dreiser his place for all time in a neat antithesis between the realism that was based on a theory of human conduct and the naturalism that reduced life to a mere animal behavior. For Dreiser this last special hell was reserved, and the jungle-like and simian activities of his characters were rather exhaustively outlined. At the time this antithesis looked silly. With the appearance of Mr. Dreiser's latest book, "A Hoosier Holiday," it becomes nonsensical. For that wise and delightful book reveals him as a very human critic of very common human life, romantically sensual and poetically realistic, with an artist's vision and a thick, warm feeling for American life.

This book gives the clue to Mr. Dreiser, to his insatiable curiosity about people, about their sexual inclinations, about their dreams, about the homely qualities that make them American. His memories give a picture of the floundering young American that is so typical as to be almost epic. No one has ever pictured this lower middle-class American life so winningly, because no one has had the necessary literary skill with the lack of self-consciousness. Mr. Dreiser is often sentimental, but it is a sentimentality that captivates you with its candor. You are seeing this vacuous, wistful, spiritually rootless, Middle-Western life through the eyes of a naïve but very wise boy. Mr. Dreiser seems queer only because he has carried along his youthful attitude in unbroken continuity. He is fascinated with sex because youth is usually obsessed with sex. He puzzles about the universe because youth usually puzzles.

He thrills to crudity and violence because sensitive youth usually recoils from the savagery of the industrial world. Imagine incorrigible, sensuous youth endowed with the brooding skepticism of the philosopher who feels the vanity of life, and you have the paradox of Mr. Dreiser. For these two attitudes in him support rather than oppose each other. His spiritual evolution was out of a pious, ascetic atmosphere into intellectual and personal freedom. He seems to have found himself without losing himself. Of how many American writers can this be said? And for this much shall be forgiven him,—his slovenliness of style, his lack of *nuances*, his apathy to the finer shades of beauty, his weakness for the mystical and the vague. Mr. Dreiser suggests the over-sensitive temperament that protects itself by an admiration for crudity and cruelty. His latest book reveals the boyhood shyness and timidity of this Don Juan of novelists. Mr. Drieser is complicated, but he is complicated in a very understandable American way, the product of the uncouth forces of small-town life and the vast disorganization of the wider American world. As he reveals himself, it is a revelation of a certain broad level of the American soul.

Mr. Dreiser seems uncommon only because he is more naïve than most of us. It is not so much that his pages swarm with sexful figures as that he rescues sex for the scheme of personal life. He feels a holy mission to slay the American literary superstition that men and women are not sensual beings. But he does not brush this fact in the sniggering way of the popular magazines. He takes it very seriously, so much so that some of his novels become caricatures of desire. It is, however, a misfortune that it has been Brieux and Freud and not native Theodore Dreiser who has saturated the sexual imagination of the younger American intelligentsia. It would have been far healthier to absorb Mr. Dreiser's literary treatment of sex than to go hysterical over its pathology. Sex has little significance unless it is treated in personally artistic, novelistic terms. The American tradition had tabooed the treatment of those infinite gradations and complexities of love that fill the literary imagination of a sensitive people. When curiosity became too strong and reticence was repealed in America, we had no means of articulating ourselves except in a deplorable pseudo-scientific jargon that has no more to do with the relevance of sex than the chemical composition of orange paint has to do with the artist's vision. Dreiser has done a real service to the American imagination in despising the underworld and going gravely to the business of picturing sex as it is lived in the personal relations of bungling, wistful, or masterful men and women. He seemed strange and rowdy only because he made sex human, and American tradition had never made it human. It had only made it either sacred or vulgar, and when these categories no longer worked, we fell under the dubious and perverting magic of the psychoanalysts.

In spite of his looseness of literary gait and heaviness of style Dreiser seems a sincere groper after beauty. It is natural enough that this should so largely be the beauty of sex. For where would a sensitive boy, brought up in Indiana and in the big American cities, get beauty expressed for him except in women? What does Mid-Western America offer to the starving except its personal beauty? A few landscapes, an occasional picture in a museum, a book of verse perhaps! Would not all the rest be one long, flaunting offense of ugliness and depression? "The 'Genius,'" instead of being that mass of pornographic horror which the Vice Societies repute it to be, is the story of a groping artist whose love of beauty runs obsessingly upon the charm of girlhood. Through different social planes, through business and manual labor and the feverish world of artists, he pursues this lure. Dreiser is refreshing in his air of the moral democrat, who sees life impassively, neither praising nor blaming, at the same time that he realizes how much more terrible and beautiful and incalculable life is than any of us are willing to admit. It may be all *apologia*, but it comes with the grave air of a mind that wants us to understand just how it all happened. "Sister Carrie" will always retain the fresh charm of a spontaneous working-out of mediocre, and yet elemental and significant, lives. A good novelist catches hold of the thread of human desire. Dreiser does this, and that is why his admirers forgive him so many faults.

If you like to speculate about personal and literary qualities that are specifically American, Dreiser should be as interesting as any one now writing in America. This becomes clearer as he writes more about his youth. His hopelessly unorientated, half-educated boyhood is so typical of the uncritical and careless society in which wistful American talent has had to grope. He had to be spiritually a self-made man, work out a philosophy of life, discover his own sincerity. Talent in America outside of the ruling class flowers very late, because it takes so long to find its bearings. It has had almost to create its own soil, before it could put in its roots and grow. It is born shivering into an inhospitable and irrelevant group. It has to find its own kind of people and piece together its links of comprehension. It is a gruelling and tedious task, but those who come through it contribute, like Vachel Lindsay, creative work that is both novel and indigenous. The process can be more easily traced in Dreiser than in almost anybody else. "A Hoosier Holiday" not only traces the personal process, but it gives the social background. The common life, as seen throughout the countryside, is touched off quizzically, and yet sympathetically, with an artist's vision. Dreiser sees the American masses in their commonness and at their pleasure as brisk, rather vacuous people, a little pathetic in their innocence of the possibilities of life and their optimistic trustfulness. He sees them ruled by great barons of industry, and yet unconscious of their serfdom. He seems to love this countryside, and he makes you love it.

Dreiser loves, too, the ugly violent bursts of American industry,—the flaming steel-mills and gaunt lakesides. "The Titan" and "The Financier" are unattractive novels, but they are human documents of the brawn of a passing

American era. Those stenographic conversations, webs of financial intrigue, bare bones of enterprise, insult our artistic sense. There is too much raw beef, and yet it all has the taste and smell of the primitive business-jungle it deals with. These crude and greedy captains of finance with their wars and their amours had to be given some kind of literary embodiment, and Dreiser has hammered a sort of raw epic out of their lives.

It is not only his feeling for these themes of crude power and sex and the American common life that makes Dreiser interesting. His emphases are those of a new America which is latently expressive and which must develop its art before we shall really have become articulate. For Dreiser is a true hyphenate, a product of that conglomerate Americanism that springs from other roots than the English tradition. Do we realize how rare it is to find a talent that is thoroughly American and wholly un-English? Culturally we have somehow suppressed the hyphenate. Only recently has he forced his way through the unofficial literary censorship. The vers-librists teem with him, but Dreiser is almost the first to achieve a largeness of utterance. His outlook, it is true, flouts the American canons of optimism and redemption, but these were never anything but conventions. There stirs in Dreiser's books a new American quality. It is not at all German. It is an authentic attempt to make something artistic out of the chaotic materials that lie around us in American life. Dreiser interests because we can watch him grope and feel his clumsiness. He has the artist's vision without the

sureness of the artist's technique. That is one of the trage-
dies of America. But his faults are those of his material
and of uncouth bulk, and not of shoddiness. He expresses
an America that is in process of forming. The interest he
evokes is part of the eager interest we feel in that growth.

The Ragged-Trousered Philanthropists
by Robert Tressall

A BOOK REVIEW

A BOOK LIKE "The Ragged-Trousered Philanthropists" reveals rather startlingly the class-bound nature of our English literature. We have no Zola, and we have practically nothing similar to that interesting autobiographical proletarian literature which one finds in France and Germany. It needs the strong, rank odor of a book like this to show us how incorrigibly "genteel" our fictional writing is, and how impossible it is for an Englishman, except at the risk of vitiating sentimentality, to interpret the life of other social classes than his own.

This book, written with the bitterness of relentless realism by a socialist house-painter in an English city, who himself struggled to the inevitable bitter end, bears in every line the stamp of autobiographical exactness. It is a little history of a short campaign in the eternal conflict between needy labor and shoddy capitalism. The wolfish competition of the workmen, the constant terror of unemployment, the petty tyranny of the foreman, the cringing servility to the employers, the secret betrayals, the speeding-up, the mean little frauds, the skimping of work—all are pictured with a remorseless veracity that is actually appalling.

The bitterness of mood in which such a book must have been written by a man who saw so intelligently the stupidities of the life around him and yet was completely unable to find any other milieu, produces fierce touches of satire. But like all good satire, its exaggerations are really searing truths. Neither his irony, nor his bitterness blinded the writer to seeing the world as it really was. That the book is veracious in atmosphere and expression, no one who has seen the deplorable frowziness of English proletarian life, or tasted that peculiar quality which makes British squalor the filthiest in the world, can doubt. This is no book for the squeamish. And yet the coarseness of British working-class life is sketched in broad strokes and outlines, rather than plastered on the canvas in the manner of a Zola; and there is a British silence as to sexuality.

If the book is not for the squeamish, it is not for the tender-hearted either. From an artistic standpoint or view, the absence of sentimentality is one of the most admirable features, but those who are accustomed to have their literature of poverty and misfortune sugared with pity and sentiment will find this unadorned veracity repulsive. The book must therefore depress and then outrage our comfortable classes. We are not accustomed to see the life of the workingman from his own point of view. Our

literature is carefully insulated from the economic interpretation of life, with its sense of the bestial struggle for
existence and its slow and interminable fight against filth
and disease. It must make our comfortable class uneasy
to see the whole remorseless mechanism of shoddy capitalism so unsparingly revealed, and to see men so palpably
the victims of economic forces. Even the most woolen-
headed of our reactionaries can hardly fail to feel the
ironic sting of the phrase, "ragged-trousered philanthropists."

Such a story is a scathing critique of the whole of British civilization, and incidentally of our own individualistic and plutocratic democracy. He must indeed be a
tough Englishman who can eat a good dinner after finish-
ing it. For the insistent fact remains that England, in spite
of her incomparable industrial wealth, the intelligence
and personal idealism of her directing classes, her free
government and humanitarian religion, has failed to secure for more than a minority of her people anything
more than a filthy caricature of human life. Up through
the beauty of park and palace rises the stench of proletarian poverty.

It is a very good thing for the world to smell that
stench. For if our directing classes and our democracy
can only once feel that evilness strongly enough, they
will begin to find it intolerable, as they have found it in
Germany, that classes should exist below a minimum
standard of life. And if we once find it intolerable we
shall set to work to make it unnecessary.

In the World of Maxim Gorky

A BOOK REVIEW

W H Y I S G O R K Y writing his autobiography with all its "oppressive horrors of our wild Russian life"? He answers his own question in the first volume,—"It is worth while because it is actual vile fact, which has not died out, even in these days—a fact which must be traced to its origin, and pulled up by the roots from the memories, the souls of the people, and from our narrow sordid lives." What that genius of his has done to this recording of actual vile fact is just what his life did to the world of his childhood. He has dominated it without distorting it, he has made it assimilable by us just as he has made his own almost intolerable boyhood into a thing of significance and growth. But these memories have the air not of being pulled up by the roots, but of being poured out in lavish abundance from one of the most sensitive and vigorous minds of our time. There is an almost oppressive fertility of offering. The incidents follow each other with their rich feeling

and suggestiveness, until one wishes for a little more interpretation, a little more universality, so that we may
know what Gorky's later life told him about the promise
of those human abysses from which he came. He does
give us one beautiful clue where he says that, although
the horrors he relates "oppress us and crush so many beautiful souls to death, yet the Russian is still so healthy and
young in heart that he can and does rise above them. For
in this amazing life of ours not only does the animal side
of our nature flourish and grow fat, but with this animal-
ism there has grown up, triumphant in spite of it, bright,
healthful and creative, a type of humanity which inspires
us to look forward to our regeneration, to the time when
we shall all live peacefully and humanly."

This we recognize as the true Russian idea which has
come to us in so many different expressions. It is this
feeling for the creative power of sheer animal life that
has kept alive so accurately in Gorky's mind what would
usually press for burial under deep layers of oblivion.
But it is wonderful that he should have come out of the
orgy of lower-class life so untainted with bitterness and
scorn. The remorseless descriptions of his people and their
fights and cruelties have nothing of harshness in them.
They are artistic truth. Few minds strike such a balance
between realism and sympathy. Gorky does not spare,
but neither does he excoriate. There is passion enough,
but it is the passion that does not spring from the effort
to feel powerful, but rather from an insatiable avidity for
life, and from an abounding humane love that is always

bursting through it. The roots of Gorky's own soul are in the endlessly vital old grandmother, with her noble speech, her forgiveness, her pleasure in the sheer sensual goodness of the world. It was out of her amazing animal-ism that there sprang the influence, "bright, healthful and creative," which gave Gorky's mind and heart the nour-ishment they needed. She did not repress the child, and her primitive vigor faced the acrid life with a warmth that kept the child from hatred. He dreaded it, he felt disgust at it, he longed to get into that truer world which came to his imagination from books. But through not hating or despising that under-life his sensitive mind was able to carry it all along with him, etched softly into the detail of these wonderful chapters, now continued in the second volume, *In the World*.

My Childhood ended with the death of the mysterious and pathetic mother. The child is sent out into the world by his grandfather to earn his living. As shopboy in a fashionable boot-shop of Nijni, as "washer-up" on a Volga steamboat, as pupil in the workshop of an ikon painter, with intervals of slavery in the house of relatives, and of freedom at home with the old grandmother, the boy's life expands like a fair and sturdy plant in a heavily manured soil. It was just as if some charmed principle of growth were driving him to fruition through this litter of demoralized lives. He keeps singularly chaste, "because the relationship of the sexes was so often and tiresomely brought to our notice in its coarsest form, and was very offensive" to him and his girl playmate.

He rebels at the stupidities of the school, but he pursues books unweariedly, with all "the burdensome humiliations, insults and alarms which his swiftly developed passion" brought him in the trivial bickering household of relatives where he worked. The Goncourts and Balzac and Walter Scott reveal to him, among the trash that he devours, a life that is better than the life he knows, with all its filth and its aimless cruelty. His good sense is irritated at the conventional novels that do nothing but reward the good and punish the wicked. He is feeling always for the truth and for his own sincerity, he is pushing out always to make emotional rapport with ideas and feelings that are like what is potential within him. This is the thread that winds through all his bitter purposeless boyhood work. And his mental loneliness is so unrelieved, except for timid contact with the apothecary who knows the meanings of words, the frail little tailor's wife who reads all day long and lends him books, and the beautiful, doubtful "Queen Margot," who has the great books for this austere and starving boy.

The search continues through his ugly life on the steamboat and in the hovels of the town, with their stream of people, preposterous and terrible, unmitigatedly frustrating. It seemed at times, Gorky says, that "a sort of dirty porridge was boiling around me, and that I was gradually being boiled away in it. Life perseveringly and roughly washed out from my soul its most delicate writings, maliciously changing them into some sort of indistinct trash, and with anger and determination I resisted its violence. I was floating on the same river as all the others, only for me the waters were colder and did not support me as easily as it did the others." But he did not sink, and his soul was not disfigured. Neither did he come out of this besotted world in any mood of complacency which, finding life too terrible to face, creates a tolerable world for its own inner fantasy of living. This is the power and wonder of his writing, that it tastes not of escape from reality and of recoil, but of grappling and absorption. Life has not washed out many writings from his soul. He seems to forget nothing. Can we believe that his impression was sensitive enough to carry along with him all this intimacy of talk and detail that he records? Well, what if we cannot? There is nothing that has not the flavor of inescapable truth, however flickering the incident. It is just the function of the literary artist that Gorky is to make everything true which he expresses. Out of the rubble of human existence his genius is building up one of the great life-stories in literature.

Our Unplanned Cities

THE CITY CLUB of a great Western town held recently a competitive exhibition of plans for a city neighborhood center. Around the walls of the beautiful corridors and rooms, designed with the last touches of thoughtful taste, were the bold conceptions of the architects of the city. Upon this problem of civic art they had lavished all their imaginative skill. These scores of radiant sketches seemed eloquent of a professional belief that for the building-up of the modern American city nothing too fine could be conceived.

Yet to see this exhibition I had had to travel from a suburban town thirty miles across a flat sandy waste strewn with the surplusage of the monster city's industry and life. We had come in the merciful dusk through an endless chaos of straggling towns, which seemed not so much towns as disgorged fragments of communities. Wilderness of dirty frame houses, gaunt factories, frowzy open spaces and outbuildings, isolated tenements in all stages of decrepitude, were interspersed with trim rows of cottages, shady streets, bright apartment-houses, and here and there an imposing church or school. From the lines of the streets one did get a certain sense of design. Otherwise the mass-effect was as if the heavens had opened and dumped out upon the desolate prairie the architectural garbage of some celestial city.

To pass from this chaotic savagery into the delightful club with its brave designs and its kindly and intelligent professional people, was to get a distinct ironic shock, a sudden sense of how little the repellent form in which the ordinary American city has got itself clothed expresses the individual intelligence and good-will of the citizens whose care should be to attend to that very civic clothing. The quality of these people, and the quality of the city as expressed in brick and wood and stone, bore not the slightest discoverable relation. One of the chief charms of a European country is the way the physical communal body of town and village seems to express the characteristic attitudes and spirit of the people. To say that the American city in its design and styles represented our spiritual capacity would be almost to say that we were a nation of madmen. We could convince a stranger that our churches and country houses were built by architects, but we could not convince him that our cities were so built.

About these confident designs there was something almost pathetic as one came into them fresh from the pervading architectural crassness. These publicists and town-planners, social workers and architects, seemed scarcely out of the magical stage. They had not yet sensed the legal and economic barriers to be surmounted for the realization of their ideals. They scarcely felt even the full incongruity of the American urban scene, which makes one perpetually wonder at the pleasantness and gentleness of the people whom one meets upon such dishevelled and barbaric streets.

I should have been more inclined to ascribe the peculiar horror of this city to its unmanageable size if I had not just come from the small capital of a neighboring state, a state which has the "social sense" if any of our states have it. Yet from a comparison of the two cities I could only conclude that the smaller had been preserved from chaos by its smallness rather than by its intelligence. On its hills by its lakes it has a famous and incomparable site, a site for artists to mould and develop. From the train one alights into an uncertain station-square, which trails off on one side to a cluster of hovels and boat-houses that obscure the lake, and on the other past an ugly line of shop-buildings towards the town. For the tree-lined lake-promenade that a Swiss town would possess, for the stately avenue to the capitol, the eye roams in vain. American towns don't have such things. I thought of the picture of this same town-approach in the report of one of those experts whom American cities suffering from twinges of town-planning conscience are calling in with increasing frequency to chide them for their sins. On the opposite page he had printed a picture of the magnificent plaza and station at San Paolo, Brazil. He had remarked that the comparison was not unfair, because both cities were small provincial capitals. It was a striking contrast of what Americans and Brazilians consider of civic importance.

Now this stodgy approach to our small Western city was no mere accident. It was more or less a clue to the town. The shabby surroundings of the capitol emphasized its showy wastefulness rather than its white grandeur. The beautiful university building on the opposite hill made one mourn the characterless streets that lay between. The lakes were almost as if they were not. The town blindly turned its back upon them all. For the lake promenades and vistas, for the stately avenues between the hills, for the harmonious city that might be there, one had to rely on one's imagination. The town straggled out feebly towards the marshes and farms. No ray of civic design or art had shone down from that great university on the hill. No effort would invest these prosaic streets with charm and significance. The people and institutions, yes! But not the civic house in which they reside.

My first city had been a vast incalculable metropolis, desolately situated, without opportunity of natural beauty. The second was the small and self-conscious capital of a self-conscious state, with a natural situation such as few towns possess. Yet apparently the same spirit had gone to the upbuilding of both. Youth and newness will scarcely explain this American idiom. The large German cities have notoriously grown faster in the last fifty years than our own. Yet they are the models of civic art and design. Many of them look in their mass-effect even newer than our American towns. Nor can it be a question of our absorption in selfish commercialism. The German people have not acquired a reputation for altruism, nor has it been the fashion to accuse their governments of Utopian idealism. That German cities are beautiful and nobly planned, and our own more hideous than anybody cares or dares to say, means that the directing and professional classes in Europe have inherited or reacquired a tradition, a town-planning sense, which we have somehow missed. Our eager pioneer development and our immigrant inundation have thrown the attention to individualistic effort, to a competitive race, and the artistic sense seems to have curiously followed. We have remained obsessed with the individual building, while the European has built towns and streets and squares rather than houses and churches and shops. The careless ugliness of the business streets and the outskirts of the American city suggests a veritable blind-spot to civic beauty. If we admitted this blindness we might wonder less frequently why we do not produce more or greater art. Youth growing up in such streets as ours would be the least likely in the world to acquire delicate discriminations, the sense of charm and atmosphere that makes for artistic sense and power.

We often excuse ourselves on the ground that our civic sense is prophetic. Where the visitor sees only the cheap prairie village, the resident sees the vision of the city which is one day to arise. When the city does arise, however, with its gridiron streets and staring blocks, one looks wistfully back to the prairie village. In too many towns this forward vision seems to have become hallucinatory.

We are still a pioneer country, sketched over rather than drawn in firm outline. But there is danger of becoming so accustomed to the pioneer stage that we forget there is no more frontier and that most of us are living in the midst of relatively old and dense communities. We have no excuse for preserving, as we do, even throughout the East, the pioneer look as of some temporary encampment. There is little inducement, it is true, to think of our cities as communal homes. Our industrial and even professional population is in constant flux. The city has become a lodging-place. We are all in this sense pioneers, scrapping our cabins, deserting our farms, and moving on to better land and fortune. But the city remains behind us, with a life and integrity of its own, regardless of the individuals who flit through it.

Until architects and engineers, school-children and the average citizen, begin to think of the town or village not merely as a geographical expression or a business enterprise, but as a communal house to be made as well-ordered and beautiful as the citizen would make his home, social effort will lack a focus, and civic good-will and enterprise be shadowy and unreal. To preach town-planning in these days of threatened municipal bankruptcy may seem like Utopianism. To emphasize this order and beauty in the face of destitution and unemployment may seem like a case of hyperaesthesia. But let us not be too sure. In Europe town-planning has gone hand in hand with the alleviation of social ills. From the chaos and ugliness of American cities flows too palpably our economic and human waste. The well-planned city pays immensely from the social point of view. In Europe it has paid immensely from the financial point of view. Perhaps the road out of bankruptcy for the American city is exactly this Utopia.

The Undergraduate

IN THESE DAYS of academic self-analysis, the intellectual caliber of the American undergraduate finds few admirers or defenders. Professors speak resignedly of the poverty of his background and imagination. Even the undergraduate himself in college editorials confesses that the student soul vibrates reluctantly to the larger intellectual and social issues of the day. The absorption in petty gossip, sports, class politics, fraternity life, suggests that too many undergraduates regard their college in the light of a glorified preparatory school where the activities of their boyhood may be worked out on a grandiose scale. They do not act as if they thought of the college as a new intellectual society in which one acquired certain rather definite scientific and professional attitudes, and learned new interpretations which threw experience and information into new terms and new lights. The average undergraduate tends to meet studies like philosophy, psychology, economics, general history, with a frankly puzzled wonder. A whole new world seems to dawn upon him, in its setting and vocabulary alien to anything in his previous life. Every teacher knows this baffling resistance of the undergraduate mind.

It is not so much that the student resists facts and details. He will absorb trusts and labor unions, municipal government and direct primaries, the poems of Matthew Arnold, and James's theory of the emotions. There is no unkindliness of his mind towards fairly concrete material. What he is more or less impervious to is points-of-view, interpretations. He seems to lack philosophy. The college has to let too many undergraduates pass out into professional and business life, not only without the germ of a philosophy, but without any desire for an interpretative clue through the maze. In this respect the American undergraduate presents a distinct contrast to the European. For the latter does seem to get a certain intellectual setting for his ideas which makes him intelligible, and gives journalism and the ordinary expression of life a certain tang which we lack here. Few of our undergraduates get from the college any such intellectual impress.

The explanation is probably not that the student has no philosophy, but that he comes to college with an unconscious philosophy so tenacious that the four years of the college in its present technique can do little to disintegrate it. The cultural background of the well-to-do American home with its "nice" people, its sentimental fiction and popular music, its amiable religiosity and vague moral optimism, is far more alien to the stern secular realism of modern university teaching than most people are willing to admit. The college world would find itself less frustrated by the undergraduate's secret hostility if it would more frankly recognize what a challenge its own attitudes are to our homely American ways of thinking and feeling. Since the college has not felt this dramatic contrast, or at least has not felt a holy mission to assail our American mushiness of thought through the undergraduate, it has rather let the latter run away with the college.

It is a trite complaint that the undergraduate takes his extra-curricular activities more seriously than his studies. But he does this because his homely latent philosophy is essentially a sporting philosophy, the good old Anglo-Saxon conviction that life is essentially a game whose significance lies in terms of winning or losing. The passion of the American undergraduate for intercollegiate athletics is merely a symbol of a general interpretation for all the activities that come to his attention. If he is interested in politics, it is in election campaigns, in the contests of parties and personalities. His parades and cheerings are the encouragement of a racer for the goal. After election, his enthusiasm collapses. His spiritual energy goes into class politics, fraternity and club emulation, athletics, every activity which is translatable into terms of winning and losing. In Continental universities this energy would go rather into a turbulence for causes and ideas, a militant radicalism or even a more militant conservatism that would send Paris students out into the streets with a "Cail-laux as-sas-sin!" or tie up an Italian town for the sake of Italia Irredenta. Even the war, though it has called out a fund of anti-militarist sentiment in the American colleges, still tends to be spoken of in terms of an international sporting event. "Who will win?" is the question here.

Now this sporting philosophy by which the American undergraduate lives, and which he seems to bring with him from his home, may be a very good philosophy for an American. It is of the same stuff with our good-humored contempt for introspection, our dread of the "morbid," our dislike of conflicting issues and insoluble problems. The sporting attitude is a grateful and easy one. Issues are decided cleanly. No irritating fringes are left over. The game is won or lost. Analysis and speculation seem superfluous. The point is that such a philosophy is as different as possible from that which motivates the intellectual world of the modern college, with its searchings, its hypotheses and interpretations and revisions, its flexibility and openness of mind. In the scientific world of the instructor, things are not won or lost. His attitude is not a sporting one.

Yet the college has allowed some of these sporting attitudes to be imposed upon it. The undergraduates' gladiatorial contests proceed under faculty supervision and patronage. Alumni contribute their support to screwing up athletic competition to the highest semi-professional pitch. They lend their hallowing patronage to fraternity life and other college institutions which tend to emphasize social distinction. And the college administration, in contrast to the European scheme, has turned the college course into a sort of race with a prize at the goal. The degree has become a sort of honorific badge for all classes of society, and the colleges have been forced to give it this quasi-athletic setting and fix the elaborate rules of the game by which it may be won—rules which shall be easy enough to get all classes competing for it, and hard enough to make it a sufficient prize to keep them all in the race. An intricate system of points and courses and examinations sets the student working for marks and the completion of schedules rather than for a new orientation in important fields of human interest.

The undergraduate can scarcely be blamed for responding to a system which so strongly resembles his sports, or for bending his energies to playing the game right, rather than assimilating the intellectual background of his teachers. So strongly has this sporting technique been acquired by the college that even when the undergraduate lacks the sporting instinct and does become interested in ideas, he is apt to find that he has only drawn attention to his own precocity and won amused notice rather than respect. In spite of the desire of instructors to get themselves over to their students, in spite of a real effort to break down the "class-consciousness" of teacher and student, the gulf between their attitudes is too fundamental to be easily bridged. Unless it is bridged, however, the undergraduate is left in a sort of Peter Pan condition, looking back to his schoolboy life and carrying along his schoolboy interests with him, instead of anticipating his graduate or professional study or his active life. What should be an introduction to professional or business life in a world of urgent political and social issues, and the ac-

workshops where theory and practice constantly fertilize each other, and where the student comes out a competent technician in his craft. But the place of the college in this scheme becomes more and more anomalous. Devoted to the traditional studies—the literatures, mathematics, philosophy, history—it is still strangely reminiscent of old musty folkways of the schoolman and theologian. Every professor knows the desire of the average student to finish his college course and grapple with his professional studies. Every professor is aware of the sharp quickening of interest which comes on entrance to the professional schools. Though part of this feeling may be due to impatience to get out into the world, much of it certainly arises from a realization that at last one has come into a sphere where thinking means action. The college, with its light and unexacting labor, is cheerfully exchanged for the grind of the professional school, because the latter touches a real world.

Whereas the higher schools give the student active work to do, almost all the methods of the college teaching conspire to force him into an attitude of passivity. The lecture system is the most impressive example of this attitude, and the lecture system seems actually to get a tightening grip upon the modern college. As standard forms have become worked out, it is customary now actually to measure the student's course by the number of hours he exposes himself to lectures. For the college course to be organized on a basis of lectures suggests that nothing has happened since Abelard spoke in Paris to twelfth-century bookless men. It is as if the magic word had still to be communicated by word of mouth, like the poems of Homer of old. The emphasis is continually upon the oral presentation of material which the professor has often himself written in a text-book, or which could be conveyed with much greater exactness and fullness from books. These books the student knows only as "collateral reading." Nothing is left undone to impress him with the idea that the books and reviews and atlases are mere subsidiaries to the thin but precious trickle of the professor's voice.

Now there may be some excuse for the lecture in a Continental university, where the professor is a personality, is not compelled to lecture, and may make of his delivery a kind of intellectual ceremony. But American professors are not only likely to be atrocious lecturers, but to hate such compulsory talking as the sheerest drudgery. Too often their own palpable derision at the artificiality of it makes the lecture an effective barrier between the student's curiosity and its satisfaction. This is not to deny that the lecture might be made into a broad interpretative survey, which would give the student the clues he needs through the maze of books. This is exactly what the best college courses tend to become. But for this the college will need interpreters, and not the humdrum recorders and collators that it has a weakness for.

The continuance of the lecture system is only symptomatic of the refusal of the college to see clearly the changing ideals of scholarship. If the student has to think

cause it to lag in the race. The reason for their persistence is, of course, that whereas the technical demands of industry and the keen emulation in the professions have sharpened the higher schools and forced a revision of ideals and methods, the practical application of the cultural studies of the college has not seemed so urgent. The turning of these cultural studies into power is to be the exact measure of our growing conviction that ideas and knowledge about social relations and human institutions are to count as urgently in our struggle with the future as any mathematical or mechanical formulas did in the development of our present.

The Uses of Infallibility

FEW PEOPLE read Newman to-day. The old anxious issues have been drowned in a flood of social problems, and that world of liberal progress which to him was the enemy at the gates has long ago broken in and carried everything before it. Newman's persuasive voice sounds thin and remote, and his ideas smell of a musty age. Yet that title of his, *Apologia Pro Vita Sua*, always intrigues one with its modern and subjective sound. It is so much what all of us are itching to write. Its egotism brushes with a faint irony that absorption in the righteousness most emphatically not ourselves with which Newman's life was mingled. In that call upon him to interpret his life, one feels an unquenchable ego which carries him over to these shameless and self-centered times. Fortunately placed for a week in a theological household, I plunged into the slightly forbidding pages of the wistful cardinal. What I found in him must be very different from what he found in himself or what anybody else found in him at the time. Newman in 1917 suggests less a reactionary theology than a subtle and secret sympa-

that killed him but Christianity. Pascal is an eternal warning from the perils of intellectual religion.

Dogma did not kill Newman, but it did not save him. He was not a pagan, but he never became a saint. He never quite got rid of dogma. And that is what so fascinates us in his religious technique. For his *Apologia* is really a subtle exposure of infallibility. It shows us what the acute intellectuality of a mystic finds to do with dogma. The goal towards which he tends is the utter bankruptcy of articulate religion. And involved in it is the bankruptcy of institutional religion. It is a religious bankruptcy that acts like modern commercial bankruptcy. All material assets are relinquished, and you start again in business on the old footing. You throw over your dogma but keep the mystic experience, which can never be taken away from you. In this way the Catholic Church becomes, or could become, eternal. Newman shows a way just short of relinquishment. He uses infallibility to liquidate his intellectual debts, and then becomes free of his creditors.

II

How these attitudes are implied in the *Apologia* I can only suggest through the surprises that a reading brought. The contention had always been that Newman's apostasy was due to feebleness of will, to a fatigue in the search for certitude that let him slip into the arms

162

of Mother Church. My Protestant training had persistently represented every going over to Rome as a surrender of individual integrity. For the sake of intellectual peace, one became content to stultify the intellect and leave all thinking to the infallible Church. There is nothing of intellectual fatigue, however, in Newman. His course did not spring from weariness of thinking. He had a most fluent and flexible mind, and if he seemed to accept beliefs at which Protestants thrilled with frightened incredulity, it was because such an acceptance satisfied some deeper need, some surer craving. Read to-day, Newman interests not because of the beliefs but because of this deeper desire. He had a sure intuition of the uses of infallibility and intellectual authority, and of their place in the scheme of things. This is his significance for the modern mind. And he is the only one of the great religious writers who seems to reach out to us and make contact with our modern attitude.

Newman loved dogma, but it was not dogma that he loved most. It was not to quiet a heart that ached with doubt that he passed from the Anglican to the Roman Church. As an Anglican Catholic he was quite as sure of his doctrine as he was as a Roman Catholic. His most primitive craving was not so much for infallibility as for legitimacy. It was because the Roman Church was primitive, legitimate, authorized, and the Anglican Church yawned in spots, that he made his reluctant choice. His Anglican brothers would not let him show them the catholicity of the Articles. They began to act schismati-

rest of the century. The Church guaranteed the established order beneath him, blotted out the sociological worries around him, and removed the incubus of dogma above him. Legitimacy and infallibility did not imprison his person or his mind. On the contrary, they freed him, because they abolished futilities from his life. Nothing is clearer from the *Apologia* than Newman's sense of the hideous vulgarity of theological discussion. He uses infallibility to purge himself of that vulgarity. He uses it in exactly the way that it should rightly be employed. The common view is that dogma is entrusted to the Church because its truth is of such momentous import as to make fatal the risk of error through private judgment. The Church is the mother who suckles us with the precious milk of doctrine without which we should die. Through ecclesiastical infallibility dogma becomes the letter and spirit of religion, bony structure and life-blood.

But Newman's use of infallibility was as a storage vault in which one puts priceless securities. They are there for service when one wishes to realize on their value. But in the business of daily living one need not look at them from one year to another. Infallibility is the strong lock of the safety-vault. It is a guarantee not of the value of the wealth but of its protection. The wealth must have other grounds for its valuableness, but one is assured that it will not be tampered with. By surrendering all your dogmas to the keeper-Church, you win, not certitude—for your treasures are no more certain inside the vault than they are in your pocket—but assurance that you will not have to see your life constantly interrupted by the need of defending them against burglars, or of proving their genuineness for the benefit of inquisitive and incredulous neighbors. The suspicion is irresistible that Newman craved infallibility not because dogma was so supremely significant to him, but because it was so supremely irrelevant. Nothing could be more revealing than his acceptance of the doctrine of the Immaculate Conception. He has no trouble whatever in believing this belated and hotly-disdained dogma. Because it is essential to his understanding of heaven and hell, eternity and the ineffable God? On the contrary, because it is so quintessentially irrelevant to anything that really entangles his emotions. His tone in acknowledging his belief is airy, almost gay. He seems to feel no implications in the belief. It merely rounds off a logical point in his theology. It merely expresses in happy metaphor a poetical truth. To him there is no tyranny in the promulgation of this new dogma. Infallibility, he seems to suggest, removes from discussion ideas that otherwise one might be weakly tempted to spend unprofitable hours arguing about.

And nothing could be more seductive than his belief in Transubstantiation. Science, of course, declares this transmutation of matter impossible. But science deals only with phenomena. Transubstantiation has to do not with phenomena but with things-in-themselves. And what has science to say about the inner reality of things?

natural. Religion becomes a village sewing-society, in which each member's life is lived in the fearful sight of all the others, while the tongues clack endlessly about rumors that can never be proved and that no one outside will ever find the slightest interest in having proved.

If the Catholic Church had used infallibility in the way that Newman did, its influence could never have been accused of oppression. There need never have been any warfare between theology and science. Infallibility affords the Church an adroit way of continuing its spiritual existence while it permits free speculation in science and ethics to go on. Suppose the Church in its infallibility had not stuck to dogma. Suppose the reformers had been successful, and the Church had accepted early scientific truth. Suppose it had refused any longer to insist on correctness in theological belief but had insisted on correctness in scientific belief. Suppose the dogmas of the Resurrection had made way for the first crude imperfect generalizations in physics. Imagine the hideousness of a world where scientific theories had been declared infallible by an all-powerful Church! Our world's safety lay exactly in the Church's rejection of science. If the Church had accepted science, scientific progress would have been impossible. Progress was possible only by ignoring the Church. Knowledge about the world could only advance through accepting gratefully the freedom which the Church tacitly offered in all that fallible field of the technique of earthly living. What progress we have we owe not to any overcoming or converting of the Church but to a scrupulous ignoring of her.

In punishing heresy the Church worked with a sound intuition. For a heretic is not a man who ignores the Church. He is one who tries to mix his theology and science. He could not be a heretic unless he were a victim of muddy thinking, and as a muddy thinker he is as much a nuisance to secular society as he is to the Church against which he rebels. He is the officious citizen who tries to break into the storage-vault with the benevolent intention of showing that the jewels are paste. But all he usually accomplishes is to set the whole town by the ears. The constructive daily life of the citizens is interrupted in a flood of idle gossip. It is as much to the interest of the intelligent authorities, who have important communal projects on hand, to suppress him as it is to the interest of the owner of the jewels. Heresy is fundamentally the error of trying to reconcile new knowledge with old dogma. The would-be heretic could far more wisely ignore theology altogether and pursue his realistic knowledge in the aloofness which it requires. If there is still any theological taint in him, he should not dabble in science at all. If there is none, the Church will scarcely feel itself threatened and he will not appear as a heretic. On the pestiferousness of the heretic both the Church and the most modern realist can agree. Let theology deal with its world of dogma. Let science deal with its world of analysable and measurable fact. Let them never touch hands or recognize even each other's existence.

litically it will appeal to the subtle who want power through the devious control over human souls. To few other types will it appeal.

Newman unveils the true paradox of dogma. If, on the one hand, you throw it open to individual judgment, you destroy it through the futile wranglings of faith which can never be objectively solved. If, on the other hand, you declare it infallible, you destroy it by slowly sending it to oblivion. Infallibility gets rid of dogma just as surely as does private judgment. Under the pretense of consolidating the Church in its cosmic rôle, Newman, therefore, has really put it in its proper parochial place as a pleasant grouping of souls who are similarly affected by a collection of beautiful and vigorous poetic ideas. Fundamentally, however, this grouping has no more universal significance than any other, than a secret society or any religious sect.

Thus Newman unconsciously anticipates the most modern realistic agnostic. For the latter would agree that to relegate dogma to the storage-vault of infallibility is exactly what ought to be done with dogma. At such an infallible as Newman pictures no modern radical need balk. Newman's argument means little more than that infallibility is merely the politest way of sending an idea to Nirvana. What more can the liberal ask who is finished with theology and all its works? He can accept this infallible in even another sense. For there is not a single Christian doctrine in which he does not feel a kind of wild accuracy. Every Christian dogma has a poetic vigor about it which might just as well be called "true" because to deny its metaphorical power would certainly be to utter an untruth. Indeed is not poetry the only "truth" that can be called infallible? For scientific truth is constantly being developed, revised, re-applied. It is only poetry that can think in terms of absolutes. Science cannot because it is experimental. But poetry may, because each soul draws its own meaning from the words. And dogma is poetry.

To render dogma infallible is to make it something that no longer has to be fought for. This attitude ultimately undermines the whole structure for belief. If it is only infallible ideas that we are to believe, then belief loses all its moral force. It is no longer a fierce struggle to maintain one's intellectual position. Nothing is at stake. One is not braced in faith with the hosts of hell assailing one's citadel. To the puritan, belief meant something to be gloweringly and tenaciously held against the world, the flesh and the devil. But Catholic belief, in the Newman atmosphere, is too sheltered, too safely insured, to count excitingly. One only yawns over it, as his own deep soul must have secretly yawned over it, and turns aside to the genuine issues of life. But this is just what we should do with belief. We are passing out of the faith era, and belief, as an intellectual attitude, has almost ceased to play an active part in our life. In the scientific attitude there is no place whatever for belief. We have no right to "believe" anything unless it has been experimentally proved. But if it has been proved, then we do not say we

What is Exploitation

M Y WESTERN FRIEND who runs a prosperous stove-factory has been finding fault with my insistent use of the word "exploitation." My outlook on life is not sufficiently cheerful, and I am inclined to see malevolence where everything is, as they say at college, healthy, hearty and happy. Our quarrel rose over the Mesaba strike, and my acceptance of an I. W. W. pamphlet as a plausible account of what was going on there. The accounts of the insecurity of pay, the petty robberies, the reeking houses, the bigoted opposition to labor organization, seemed to me to smell of truth, because I had read the maddening tales of Colorado and West Virginia, and seen with my own eyes in Scranton and Gary and Pittsburgh the way workers live, not in crises of industrial war but in brimming times of peace.

My friend, however, is more robust. He would make no such hasty impassioned judgments. He would judge nothing without "going to the mines, working in them for a year or two, being one of the men, getting their free confidence, then working for a couple of years as confidential auditor for the company." Such Olympian judiciality fills me with envy and dismay. I feel that his serenity is the normal mood of healthy activity, facing the modern world. Could he find anything but scorn for those of us who go around with the vestiges of what it is now priggish to call a "social conscience?" To him an industrial strike is like an exciting political contest or the recriminations between "two kid baseball teams." Both sides, he says, "squawk a good deal about the raw stuff the other side is trying to pull off," but deep down, his experience convinces him, "they are very uniformly a pretty human bunch." He hasn't been to Mesaba, but his friend the Duluth bread-dealer assures him that agitators were the cause of all the trouble. They always are. Trouble, to my friend, is a personal matter. He sees individuals, laboring as happily as they can expect to labor on this far from perfumed earth. He sees their contentment disturbed by "outsiders," individuals, bitter envious mischievous men who make a business of setting workmen against their employers. He sees the "outsiders" deluding, persuading, intimidating honest workers into stopping work and engaging in careers of lawlessness. He sees the individual employer in natural self-defense fighting for his rights, defending his property, ousting the agitators, carrying the war into his laborers' camp. From the busy office of his stove-factory, it all looks like a personal quarrel between free and equal individuals. When the state interferes with its militia and its injunctions, it is not flouting individuality, but merely doing its business of maintaining order and defending private property.

toward weakening his pull, and lessening the amount he was able to skim. He was not robbing me, and no person of sense would have said he was, but our very relation was an exploitation. There was no medium way between exploitation and philanthropy.

My stove-factory friend, however, will have none of this theory. If it is a question of power, he says, then Mike Solomon exploits the stove company when he is able to get $3 a day, on account of the present demand for labor, when $2 was wealth to him a year ago. Then I admit that local groups of workers are able—either through lack of competition or clever politics or display of force—to exercise temporarily a decisive pull on the surplus and divert most of it to themselves. It is all a question of power. But as long, I tell him, as the employer is entrenched in property rights with the armed state behind him, the power will be his, and the class that does the diverting will not be labor. My friend, however, does not like these Nietzschean terms. He is sure that his workmen have just as much power to exploit him as he has of exploiting them. This is where we differ, and this is why thought will buzz in an angry murky haze over eight-hour bills and individual contracts and collective bargaining as long as millions agree with him. He trusts rights, I trust power. He recognizes only individuals, I recognize classes.

That is why I can never make him understand what I mean by "exploitation." He thinks of it as something personally brutal. He does not see it inherent in a system, for which no one is "specifically to blame" only because all are equally guilty of short vision and flimsy analysis. And yet as I read his letters and clippings, I wonder if he is not the realist and I the mystic. He punctures my phrases of power and class with a coarse satisfied Hunky to whom work and disease and riot are all in the day's work and who would despise the philosophy which I am so anxiously weaving for him. It seems a long way from my dainty music-bench to the iron range, or the stove-factory. One has to feel exploitation perhaps before one understands it. I console myself with the thought that power is itself mystic, and that my friend will have to get hit with some invisible threat of class-force, as some of his frightened friends are now getting hit, before he will analyze any deeper that industrial system of which he is so efficient and loyal an officer.

Those Columbia Trustees

A LETTER TO THE EDITOR OF THE NEW REPUBLIC

October, 1917

SIR:

In summarily dismissing Professors Cattell and Dana, the trustees of Columbia University have not preserved themselves from speedy and caustic protest. Already three of the most distinguished professors have criticised this action before their classes; two student petitions are under way; and alumni who are jealous of academic freedom are interesting themselves in the matter. It is clear now that the so-called "inquisition" into the "state of teaching at the University," which aroused so much amusement and resentment last spring, was seriously meant as a tool to dislodge professors who held unpopular opinions. An attempt has been made by the university to give a democratic flavor to this dismissal. But the only evidence offered as to "the judgment of the faculties" turns out to be a letter from eight members of the Committee of Instruction of the Faculty of Applied Science, with the work of which department neither Professor Cattell nor Professor Dana were in any way connected. This committee constitutes but a small minority of the Faculty of Applied Science, which in turn constitutes only a small minority of the faculty of the University. The faculty as a whole was not consulted, nor did it take any action whatever in the case. The trustees did not even accept the recommendations of the so-called Committee of Nine which "coöperated" with the trustees in the "inquisition," and indirectly represented the faculty. These arbitrary dismissals, therefore, were accomplished, under the plea of war urgency, in exactly the manner which has aroused so much protest in recent years and which has led to the formation of an Association of University Professors to safeguard the rights of academic freedom. The treatment of Professor Dana is particularly flagrant. He is a capable scholar, and a most excellent and popular teacher· There was no charge that he had neglected his duties, or intruded his opinions into his college work, or let his political activities detract from his service to the University. The only charge was that he had associated during the summer with "disloyal" individuals and organizations, thus doing grave injury to the university which he represented. No proof whatever is presented by President Butler as to the dangerous nature of the People's Council with which Professor Dana has been associated. It is by the irresponsible newspapers and not by the government that the Council and its leaders have been convicted for obstructing the war. The university is therefore in the awkward position of discharging a "treasonable" professor for mere association with an organization which in the eyes of a vigilant government is still law-abiding and free from prosecution. President Butler has been willing to use newspaper chatter as evidence for finding that "the gravest damage" has been inflicted upon the good name and influence of Columbia University by Professor Dana. What is the nature of this damage? No damage done to the university in the minds of the readers of the irresponsible and irrational press can equal the damage done in the minds of all fair-thinking men and women by this callous violation by the Columbia trustees of the principles of academic freedom. The case the university makes out for itself is so flimsy that only one conclusion is possible. Columbia has deprived itself of an honorable and valuable teacher, because he had opinions and engaged in activities which were unpopular. A similar proscription has been going on in many other American colleges. Yet if academic freedom is to be anything more than a name, college authorities must learn to tolerate unpopular opinion. If the good name and influence of Columbia is so fragile and insecure that it can be seriously impaired by the political heresies of two professors out of the hundreds, then the sooner the university closes its doors the better. One word of defiance to this outside clamor which university authorities pretend to take so seriously would silence it. One courageous instance of the protection of a heretical professor would give the university a moral prestige that would be unassailable. Particularly in war time is it essential that the university should not be swayed by the passion and prejudice of the hour. Unless a university teacher may hold opinions different from what the university as an institution holds, he is not intellectually free. Professor Dana's only offense was that he retained his pacific and internationalist philosophy in war time, and associated with other radicals who had retained theirs. He felt himself, as President Butler admits, to be actuated by the highest patriotic motives. He was charged with no specific offense against his country. The only charge is nonconformity. The Association of University Professors has never had a clearer case on which to base a fight for the principles of academic freedom.

A Moral Equivalent for
Universal Military Service

July, 1916

THE CURRENT AGITATION for preparedness has
set hosts of Americans to thinking out for the first time
what a real national strength and readiness would mean.
We suddenly realize that if we are to defeat that militaristic trend which we loathe we shall have to offer some
kind of action more stirring and more creative. The call
now upon every citizen is to be not nebulously patriotic,
but clear and lucid as to America's aims, so that our national energy shall not be squandered and misused. There
looms up as a crucial need that "moral equivalent for war"
with which William James first roused our imaginations.
It seems no longer so academic a proposal. Confronted
with the crisis, we see that he analyzed the situation with
consummate accuracy.

All around us we feel a very genuine craving for unity
of sentiment, for service, for some new national lift and
broadening which shall keep us out of the uneasy petti-
ness into which the American conscience has threatened

to fall. In our hearts we know that to crystallize this desire into a meaningless sentiment, or into a piling-up of armaments or a proscribing of alien cultures, would not satisfy us, We want action, but we do not want military action. Even the wildest patriots know that America would have to go through the most pernicious and revolutionary changes to accept the universal military service which they advocate. We wish to advance from where we stand. We begin to suspect that military service, flag-reverence, patriotic swagger, are too much the weary old deep-dug channels into which national feeling always runs and is lost. The flooding river fills again its archaic and forsaken paths. Our present confusion expresses the dilemma we find ourselves in, when our instincts impel us into courses that our intelligence tells us we ought not to follow.

Our American danger is not so much that we become militarists as that we grope along, fretting and harrying each other into a unity which is delusive, and expressing our "Americanism" in activities that are not creative. The best will in America at the present time seems to crave some kind of national service but it veers off from military service. Until we satisfy that craving, we shall run at halfpower, and suffer all the dissatisfaction and self-despising that comes from repressed energy. The question which all are asking, in the varied and disguised forms, is: How can we all together serve America by really enhancing her life?

To more and more of us the clue has come through

James's conception of a productive army of youth, warring against nature and not against men, finding in drudgery and toil and danger the values that war and preparation for war had given. Ten years ago such an army seemed Utopian. We had neither the desire nor the technique. It seemed a project not to be realized without a reorganization of our life so radical as to make the army itself unnecessary. To-day, however, a host of new attitudes seem to give us the raw material out of which such a national service could be created. We hear much of universal military service as "educational." The Plattsburgs are sugar-coated as "civic training camps," "schools for citizenship." Universal service no longer stands on its old ground of mere preparation for war. It is frankly trying to get itself recognized as an indispensable mode of education. The next pertinent step is evidently to ask why, if universal service is valuable because it is educational, it should not be constructed on a strict educational foundation.

James's proposal sounded Utopian because it would require an entirely new and colossal national organization to put it into action. Universal military service in this country would certainly mean such a task. But if our national service is to be educational, we already have the organization existence. The rapidly consolidating public school systems in the states provide the machinery for such an organization. As the public schools become better places for children to spend their time in, we are growing less tolerant of the forms of schooling outside of the public system. The tendency is towards the inclusion of all children in the public school. And the progressive states are requiring schooling up to the full age of sixteen years. We are rapidly creating a public school system, effectively administered by the states, which gives us the one universally national, compulsory service which we possess or are ever likely to consent to.

Education is the only form of "conscription" to which Americans have ever given consent. Compulsory military service would require decades of Napoleonic political evangelism to introduce. Compulsory education is universally accepted. For a national service which shall be educational you would have to convert nobody. The field is sown. No one denies the right of the state to conscript the child for education. But coupled with this assent is the insistence that the education shall be the freest, and most stimulating that we know how to give. The current educational interest arises largely from the indignant demand that a state which takes all the children must meet the needs of every child. The very recent enthusiasm for "vocational education" means that we want a schooling that shall issue in capacity for fruitful occupation. A national educational service could give training for work at the same time that it gave opportunity for service.

It is only a national service of this kind that would really be universal. Military service is a sham universality. It omits the feminine half of the nation's youth. And of the masculine half it uses only the physically best. France is the only country where the actual levy on men for military service has approximated the number liable. But worst of all, military service irons out all differences of talent and ability. It does not even tap the resources it enlists. It makes out of an infinitely varied group a mere machine of uniform, obeying units. The personal qualities, the individual powers of the youth it trains, are of no relevance whatever. Men are valuable exactly to the degree that they crush out these differences.

A national service for education would not be a sham. It would actually enlist the coöperation of every youth and girl. It would aim at stimulation, not obedience. It would call out capacity and not submerge it. It would organize varied tasks adapted to the capacities and strengths of its young citizenry. It would be universal, but it would be compulsory only in the sense that it called every one to the service. The tasks would not be enforced drudgery, but work that enlisted the will and toned up the aspirations.

Such a national service would be the logical outgrowth of our public school system. Suppose the state said: All children shall remain in school till the age of sixteen years. Between the ages of sixteen and twenty-one they shall spend two years in national service. This service shall be organized and administered by the state educational administrations, but supervised and subsidized by the national government. The service would be performed as national service, but its work would be constructive and communal in its purposes and not military. Special training could be given as a branch of this service to those who were best fitted for it. But defense would be but an incident in our constructive life, and not the sinew of our effort.

The tasks for such a national service would evidently be different from those contemplated by James. He thought of turning his army of youth into the drudgery of the world, where they might win in heroic toil and self-sacrifice the moral rewards which war had formerly given. But if our service is to be universal, it cannot be mere unskilled labor in mines and farms and forests. A large proportion of our youth would be disqualified. Furthermore, a service which made such frontal attack on industry would be bitterly resisted by those with whom its work competed. We are not prepared for a service which clashes too suddenly and harshly with the industrial system. What we need is a service which shall not so much do the old work of the world as create new demands and satisfy them. This national service could do the things which need to be done, but which are not now being done. It could have for its aim the improvement of the quality of our living. Our appalling slovenliness, the ignorance of great masses in city and country as to the elementary technique of daily life—this should be the enemy of the army of youth. I have a picture of a host of eager youth missionaries swarming over the land, spreading the health knowledge, the knowledge of domestic science, of gardening, of tastefulness, that they have learned in school.

Such a service would provide apprentices for communal services in town and country, as many schools and colleges are already actually providing. Food inspection, factory inspection, organized relief, the care of dependents, playground service, nursing in hospitals—all this would be a field for such an educational service. On a larger scale, tree-planting, the care and repair of roads, work on conservation projects, the care of model farms, would be tasks for this army. As I was burning caterpillars' nests the other day in New Jersey and saw the trees sinister with grey webs, I thought of the destroying army of youth that should be invading the land clearing it of all insect pests. We might even come to the forcible rebuilding of the slovenly fences and outhouses which strew our landscape, and to an imposition of cleanness upon our American countryside. With an army of youth we could perform all those services of neatness and mercy and intelligence which our communities now know how to perform and mean to perform, but have not the weapons to wield.

The army could be organized in flying squadrons, so that its youth could travel widely and see and serve all kinds of men and communities. For its direction we would need that new type of teacher-engineer-community worker that our best school systems are already producing. Scientific schools, schools of philanthropy, are turning out men and women who could step into their places as non-commissioned officers for such an army. The service could be entirely flexible. Boys and girls could learn the rudiments of their trade or profession in actual service with the army. Book studies could be carried on, and college learning could come to its own as the intellectual fertilizer of a wholesome and stimulating life. Athletics and sports would be an integral part of the two years' service. There would be long periods of camping in the national parks or upon ocean beaches. The Boy Scouts and Camp-Fire Girls already give the clue to such an enterprise.

If objection is made that this national educational service would fail to bring out the sterner qualities of heroism and self-sacrifice, and would not be a genuine moral equivalent for war, the answer is that the best kind of a moral equivalent is a moral sublimation. We want to turn the energies of youth away from their squandering in mere defense or mere drudgery. Our need is to learn how to live rather than die; to be teachers and creators, not engines of destruction; to be inventors and pioneers, not mere defenders. Our cities and isolated farms alike are mute witnesses that Americans have never learned how to live. Suppose we had a national service which was making a determined assault for the enhancement of living. Would its standards and discipline be less rigorous? Rather would the ingenuity and imagination have to be of the finest.

Some such conception of national service is the only one which will give us that thrill of unity and vigor which we seek. An educational service built on the public school system puts the opportunity in our hands. The raw material in attitudes and desires is here. Every task that an army of youth might perform is already being done in some school or college or communal service. All we need to do is to coördinate and make universal what is now haphazard and isolated. An army of youth which focused school work would provide just that purpose that educators seek. The advocates of "preparedness" are willing to spend billions on a universal military service which is neither universal nor educational nor productive. Cannot we begin to organize a true national service which will let all serve creatively towards the toning up of American life?

Conscience and Intelligence
in War

September, 1917

THE MERELY "conscientious objector" has absorbed
too much attention from those who are concerned about
understanding the non-popularity of our participation in
the war. Not all the pacifist feeling has had an evangelical
color. There is an element of anti-war sentiment which has
tried to be realistic, and does not hope to defeat war
merely by not doing something. Though events have been
manipulated against it, this element neither welcomes mar-
tyrdom nor hopes to be saved for its amiable sentiments.
And it is just this attitude, far more significantly "American" than "conscientious objection," that John Dewey
has ignored in his recent article on "Conscience and Compulsion." The result has been to apply his pragmatic philosophy in its least convincing form.

His criticism is of the merely good and merely conscientious souls whose moral training has emphasized
sentiments rather than specific purposes, and who are always found helpless before the coercion of events. His

argument follows the well-known lines of his instrumental use of the intelligence for the realization of conscious social purpose. The conscience, he implies, is balked by an unpleasant situation, is futile unless it attaches itself to forces moving in another, and more desirable, direction. Dissatisfied with the given means or end, one chooses another alternative, either a new end to which the means may be shaped, or a new means to effect the desired end. But in applying this theory to the war situation, does not the philosopher ignore the fact that it is exactly in war that alternatives are rigorously limited? Is not war perhaps the one social absolute, the one situation where the choice of ends ceases to function? Obviously in a world of choice one may hope intelligently to select and manipulate some social mechanism by which a desired social arrangement may be brought about. But war always comes to seem just that urgent, inevitable crisis of the nation's life where everything must be yielded to one purpose. For a few months, the public may retain the illusion of freedom, of mastery over social forces. But as war continues, there comes the deep popular recognition that there is now but one end—victory; and one means—the organization of all the resources of the nation into a conventional war technique. "Peace without victory" becomes a logical and biological contradiction. Belligerent peoples will have long ago realized that war is its own end, and that, to paraphrase a popular ditty, they fight because they fight because they fight. This was the real basis of the opposition to the President's gesture for peace—the realization that though America might still be living in a pragmatic world, war had made Europe a realm of the absolute. And in our own country, war had not been with us for ten weeks before "peace without victory" changed officially into "conquer or submit!"

In wartime, there is literally no other end but war, and the objector, therefore, lives no longer with a choice of alternatives. The pacifist conscience attaches itself to no end because no end exists which connects with its desires. Plans and programmes may exist which have not to do with war, but they exist only in the realm of fantasy, not in the realm of practical politics. Peace comes through victory or exhaustion, and not through creative intelligence. The appeal to force removes everything automatically to a non-intelligent sphere of thinking and acting. Mr. Dewey is depressed at the number of conscientious young men who exchanged their "Thou shalt not kill" into an "Obey the law," though they saw the situation exactly as before. But his depression is due only to that inexorability which every pragmatist must resent. It is not just to be depressed at their poverty of imagination. For he is dealing with precisely the one situation in which his philosophy will no longer work. He implies that there was some way by which conscience could operate very differently from that whose main concern is to "remain itself unspotted from within." Well, in what way? Where does one find "forces moving in another direction"? One may find forces moving against the war, resisting the organization for war, agitating for a speedy peace. But such forces are not merely alternative social policies. They are not morally equivalent to the policy of war. They have the unique quality of disloyalty. They challenge the entire force of the nation. As soon as they threaten to become at all effective, they are automatically crushed out, under even the most democratic of governments. Never has a government in wartime been known to refuse the use of relentless coercion against "forces moving in another direction." The attaching of one's conscience to any such forces is infallibly taken to be the allying of oneself with the disloyal, and the inadvertent aiding of the nation's enemies. There is, of course, the alternative of revolution, which would have much the same effect as disloyalty. Does Mr. Dewey mean to urge the "conscientious objector" to take to disloyalty or revolution in his efforts to attach his conscience to intelligent alternatives? And if not, will he tell us what social mechanism he knows of that is considered relevant or even permissible in wartime that does not contribute to the war technique? One resists or one obeys. If one resists, one is martyred or coerced. If one obeys, the effect is just as if one accepted the war.

In wartime, then, one's pragmatic conscience moves in a vacuum. There is no leverage to clutch. To a philosopher of the creative intelligence, the fact that war blots out the choice of ends and even of means should be the final argument against its use as a technique for any purpose whatever. War once entered upon, neither means nor ends can really be revised or altered. The acceptance of the war by Mr. Dewey can only be explained by the prevailing sentiment that this was a war in which we had to be. I have heard him say that it was far better to enter the war intelligently than blindly or hysterically. This is not quite the same as saying that deliberate murder is more creatively intelligent than murder committed in the heat of sudden passion. For what Mr. Dewey meant was probably that if we entered the war intelligently we would choose the ends which the war technique might serve. But is it not a little curious to find the men who thought the war inevitable—"what could we do?"—and who could neither prevent it nor devise an alternative, still confident that they can control its terrible force for beneficent purposes? Having accepted the inevitable of war, one can more easily accept other inevitables.

At the back of Mr. Dewey's mind was perhaps the hope that the pacifist conscience, through hating war and everything connected with it, might aid this war because of the radical social reforms it was sure to bring. But the same people who thought of this as an end for which the pacifist should be willing to accept the instrument, are now complaining that labor, though it consecrated itself to the nation's service, is not now receiving the nation's gratitude; that the war-swollen fortune is sliding free of paying for the war; that education is being impoverished, and national demoralization rather than integration taking place. These ironic frustrations of the social purpose were foreseen by the realistic pacifists. They were the best of reasons for finding an alternative to war. They were the best of motives for not attaching one's conscience to forces that involved a technique which infallibly trailed along these social evils. Once you accept war, there is no choice but to be shoved along the line of inevitables with which war is organically bound up.

In wartime, therefore, the "forces moving in another direction" to which Mr. Dewey invites the objecting conscience to attach itself, are illusory. War is just that absolute situation which is its own end and its own means, and which speedily outstrips the power of intelligent and creative control. As long as you are out of war, events remain to some degree malleable. This was the argument for "armed neutrality." But clamp down the psychic pattern of war on the nation, and you have precipitated an absolute where mastery becomes a mockery. Mere conscientious objection in wartime is not so uncreative or unintelligent as Mr. Dewey represents it. No social machinery exists to make dissent effective. Alternative ends are illusory. You can only accept, or rebel, or remain apathetic. This is not true of other social situations. It is true of war. If you are skeptical of the technique of war, or of the professional aims, a negative attitude is the only possible one. It may not be noble to concentrate on your own integrity, but it is perhaps better than to be a hypocrite or a martyr. And if pragmatists like Mr. Dewey are going to accept "inevitables," you at least have an equal right to choose what shall seem inevitable to you.

To many pragmatists the impotence of the pacifists in the period preceding the war has been a sore point. They are scolded for their lack of organization and their mere obstructiveness. Actually, they were fertile in constructive suggestions. But no social machinery existed for harnessing their conscience to action. The referendum would have been a slight democratic clutch. It was hooted out of court. Armed neutrality was foozled. The forces that were irresistibly for war had control of the war-making machinery. The pacifists sounded ridiculous and unreasonable, because the drive was the other way. The war suction had begun. Choices were already abolished, and the most realistic and constructive pacifism in the world would have been helpless.

In all this chain of events, those minds were able to retain a feeling of alternative forces and of free choice which were in sympathy with the announced purpose of the war and not temporarily hostile to its technique. The philosophy of creative intelligence still seemed to be working because there was no need to test its applicability. The dissenter, however, felt cruelly the coercive forces. Suppose I really believe that world peace will more likely come exactly "by not doing something," by a collusive neglect of imperialistic policy on the new Russian model. Suppose I believe that a federalism of sovereign nations will only mean more competitive wars. What forces are there then to which I can assimilate this war of ours, and so make my intelligence and conscience count for what little they may? Is not Mr. Dewey's case against the merely passive built on an assumption that if one chose freely one would choose the present inevitable forces? But the mind that is skeptical of these present forces,—is it not thrown back to a choice of resistance or apathy? Can one do more than wait and hope for wisdom when the world becomes pragmatic and flexible again?

The War and The Intellectuals

June, 1917

To those of us who still retain an irreconcilable animus against war, it has been a bitter experience to see the unanimity with which the American intellectuals have thrown their support to the use of war-technique in the crisis in which America found herself. Socialists, college professors, publicists, new-republicans, practitioners of literature, have vied with each other in confirming with their intellectual faith the collapse of neutrality and the riveting of the war-mind on a hundred million more of the world's people. And the intellectuals are not content with confirming our belligerent gesture. They are now complacently asserting that it was they who effectively willed it, against the hesitation and dim perceptions of the American democratic masses. A war made deliberately by the intellectuals! A calm moral verdict, arrived at after a penetrating study of inexorable facts! Sluggish masses, too remote from the world-conflict to be stirred, too lacking in intellect to perceive their danger! An alert intellectual class, saving the people in spite of themselves, biding their time with Fabian strategy until the nation could be moved into war without serious resistance! An intellectual class, gently guiding a nation through sheer force of ideas into what the other nations entered only through predatory craft or popular hysteria or militarist madness! A war free from any taint of self-seeking, a war that will secure the triumph of democracy and inter-nationalize the world! This is the picture which the more self-conscious intellectuals have formed of themselves, and which they are slowly impressing upon a population which is being led no man knows whither by an indubitably intellectualized President. And they are right, in that the war certainly did not spring from either the ideals or the prejudices, from the national ambitions or hysterias, of the American people, however acquiescent the masses prove to be, and however clearly the intellectuals prove their putative intuition.

Those intellectuals who have felt themselves totally out of sympathy with this drag toward war will seek some explanation for this joyful leadership. They will want to understand this willingness of the American intellect to open the sluices and flood us with the sewage of the war spirit. We cannot forget the virtuous horror and stupefaction which filled our college professors when they read the famous manifesto of their ninety-three German colleagues in defense of their war. To the American academic mind of 1914 defense of war was inconceivable. From Bernhardi it recoiled as from a blasphemy, little dreaming that two years later would find it creating its own cleanly reasons for imposing military service on the country and for talking of the rough rude currents of health and regeneration that war would send through the American body politic. They would have thought any one mad who talked of shipping American men by the hundreds of thousands—conscripts—to die on the fields of France. Such a spiritual change seems catastrophic when we shoot our minds back to those days when neutrality was a proud thing. But the intellectual progress has been so gradual that the country retains little sense of the irony. The war sentiment, begun so gradually but so perseveringly by the preparedness advocates who came from the ranks of big business, caught hold of one after another of the intellectual groups. With the aid of Roosevelt, the murmurs became a monotonous chant, and finally a chorus so mighty that to be out of it was at first to be disreputable and finally almost obscene. And slowly a strident rant was worked up against Germany which compared very creditably with the German fulminations against the greedy power of England. The nerve of the war-feeling centered, of course, in the richer and older classes of the Atlantic seaboard, and was keenest where there were French or English business and particularly social connections. The sentiment then spread over the country as a class-phenomenon, touching everywhere those upperclass elements in each section who identified themselves with this Eastern ruling group. It must never be forgotten that in every community it was the least liberal and least democratic elements among whom the preparedness and later the war sentiment was found. The farmers were apathetic, the small business men and workingmen are still apathetic towards the war. The election was a vote of confidence of these latter classes in a President who would keep the faith of neutrality. The intellectuals, in other words, have identified themselves with the least democratic forces in American life. They have assumed the leadership for war of those very classes whom the American democracy has been immemorially fighting. Only in a world where irony was dead could an intellectual class enter war at the head of such illiberal cohorts in the avowed cause of world-liberalism and world-democracy. No one is left to point out the undemocratic nature of this war-liberalism. In a time of faith, skepticism is the most intolerable of all insults.

Our intellectual class might have been occupied, during the last two years of war, in studying and clarifying the ideals and aspirations of the American democracy, in discovering a true Americanism which would not have been merely nebulous but might have federated the different ethnic groups and traditions. They might have spent the time in endeavoring to clear the public mind of the cant of war, to get rid of old mystical notions that clog our thinking. We might have used the time for a great wave of education, for setting our house in spiritual order. We could at least have set the problem before ourselves. If our intellectuals were going to lead the administration, they might conceivably have tried to find some way of securing peace by making neutrality effective. They might have turned their intellectual energy not to the problem of jockeying the nation into war, but to the problem of using our vast neutral power to attain democratic ends for the rest of the world and ourselves without the use of the malevolent technique of war. They might have failed. The point is that they scarcely tried. The time was spent not in clarification and education, but in a mulling over of nebulous ideals of democracy and liberalism and civilization which had never meant anything fruitful to those ruling classes who now so glibly used them, and in giving free rein to the elementary instinct of self-defense. The whole era has been spiritually wasted. The outstanding feature has been not its Americanism but its intense colonialism. The offense of our intellectuals was not so much that they were colonial—for what could we expect of a nation composed of so many national elements?—but that it was so one-sidedly and partisanly colonial. The official, reputable expression of the intellectual class has been that of the English colonial. Certain portions of it have been even more loyalist than the King, more British even than Australia. Other colonial attitudes have been vulgar. The colonialism of the other American stocks was denied a hearing from the start. America might have been made a meeting-ground for the different national attitudes. An intellectual class, cultural colonists of the different European nations, might have threshed out the issues here as they could not be threshed out in Europe. Instead of this, the English colonials in university and press took command at the start, and we became an intellectual Hungary where thought was subject to an effective process of Magyarization. The reputable opinion of the American intellectuals became more and more either what could be read pleasantly in London, or what was written in an earnest effort to put Englishmen straight on their war-aims and war-technique. This Magyarization of thought produced as a counter-reaction a peculiarly offensive and inept German apologetic, and the two partisans divided the field between them. The great masses, the other ethnic groups, were inarticulate. American public opinion was almost as little prepared for war in 1917 as it was in 1914.

The sterile results of such an intellectual policy are inevitable. During the war the American intellectual class has produced almost nothing in the way of original and illuminating interpretation. Veblen's "Imperial Germany"; Patten's "Culture and War," and addresses; Dewey's "German Philosophy and Politics"; a chapter or two in Weyl's "American Foreign Policies";—is there much else of creative value in the intellectual repercussion of the war? It is true that the shock of war put the American intellectual to an unusual strain. He had to sit idle and think as spectator not as actor. There was no government to which he could docilely and loyally tender his mind as did the Oxford professors to justify England in her own eyes. The American's training was such as to make the fact of war almost incredible. Both in his reading of history and in his lack of economic perspective he was badly prepared for it. He had to explain to himself something which was too colossal for the modern mind, which outran any language or terms which we had to interpret it in. He had to expand his sympathies to the breaking-point, while pulling the past and present into some sort of interpretative order. The intellectuals in the fighting countries had only to rationalize and justify what their country was already doing. Their task was easy. A neutral, however, had really to search out the truth. Perhaps perspective was too much to ask of any mind. Certainly the older colonials among our college professors let their prejudices at once dictate their thought. They have been comfortable ever since. The war has taught them nothing and will teach them nothing. And they have had the satisfaction, under the rigor of events, of seeing prejudice submerge the intellects of their younger colleagues. And they have lived to see almost their entire class, pacifists and democrats too, join them as apologists for the "gigantic irrelevance" of war.

We have had to watch, therefore, in this country the same process which so shocked us abroad,—the coalescence of the intellectual classes in support of the military programme. In this country, indeed, the socialist intellectuals did not even have the grace of their German brothers and wait for the declaration of war before they broke for cover. And when they declared for war they showed how thin was the intellectual veneer of their socialism. For they called us in terms that might have emanated from any bourgeois journal to defend democracy and civilization, just as if it was not exactly against those very bourgeois democracies and capitalist civilizations that socialists had been fighting for decades. But so subtle is the spiritual chemistry of the "inside" that all this intellectual cohesion—herd-instinct become herd-intellect —which seemed abroad so hysterical and so servile, comes to us here in highly rational terms. We go to war to save the world from subjugation! But the German intellectuals went to war to save their culture from barbarization! And the French went to war to save their beautiful France! And the English to save international honor! And Russia, most altruistic and self-sacrificing of all, to save a small State from destruction! Whence is our miraculous intuition of our moral spotlessness? Whence our confidence that history will not unravel huge economic and imperialist forces upon which our rationalizations float like bubbles? The Jew often marvels that his race alone should have been chosen as the true people of the cosmic God. Are not our intellectuals equally fatuous when they tell us that our war of all wars is stainless and thrillingly achieving for good?

An intellectual class that was wholly rational would have called insistently for peace and not for war. For months the crying need has been for a negotiated peace, in order to avoid the ruin of a deadlock. Would not the same amount of resolute statesmanship thrown into intervention have secured a peace that would have been a subjugation for neither side? Was the terrific bargaining power of a great neutral ever really used? Our war followed, as all wars follow, a monstrous failure of diplomacy. Shamefacedness should now be our intellectuals' attitude, because the American play for peace was made so little more than a polite play. The intellectuals have still to explain why, willing as they now are to use force to continue the war to absolute exhaustion, they were not willing to use force to coerce the world to a speedy peace.

Their forward vision is no more convincing than their past rationality. We go to war now to internationalize the world! But surely their League to Enforce Peace is only a palpable apocalyptic myth, like the syndicalists' myth of the "general strike." It is not a rational programme so much as a glowing symbol for the purpose of focusing belief, of setting enthusiasm on fire for international order. As far as it does this it has pragmatic value, but as far as it provides a certain radiant mirage of idealism for this war and for a world-order founded on mutual fear, it is dangerous and obnoxious. Idealism should be kept for what is ideal. It is depressing to think that the prospect of a world so strong that none dare challenge it should be the immediate ideal of the American intellectual. If the League is only a makeshift, a coalition into which we enter to restore order, then it is only a description of existing fact, and the idea should be treated as such. But if it is an actually prospective outcome of the settlement, the keystone of American policy, it is neither realizable nor desirable. For the programme of such a League contains no provision for dynamic national growth or for international economic justice. In a world which requires recognition of economic internationalism far more than of political internationalism, an idea is reactionary which proposes to petrify and federate the nations as political and economic units. Such a scheme for international order is a dubious justification for American policy. And if American policy had been sincere in its belief that our participation would achieve international beatitude, would we not have made our entrance into the war conditional upon a solemn general agreement to respect in the final settlement thse principles of international order? Could we have afforded, if our war was to end war by the establishment of a league of honor, to risk the defeat of our vision and our betrayal in the settlement? Yet we are in the war, and no such solemn agreement was made, nor has it ever been suggested.

The case of the intellectuals seems, therefore, only very speciously rational. They could have used their energy to force a just peace or at least to devise other means than war for carrying through American policy. They could have used their intellectual energy to ensure that our participation in the war meant the international order which they wish. Intellect was not so used. It was used to lead an apathetic nation into an irresponsible war, without guarantees from those belligerents whose cause we were saving. The American intellectual, therefore, has been rational neither in his hindsight nor his foresight. To explain him we must look beneath the intellectual reasons to the emotional disposition. It is not so much what they thought as how they felt that explains our intellectual class. Allowing for colonial sympathy, there was still the personal shock in a world-war which outraged all our preconceived notions of the way the world was tending. It reduced to rubbish most of the humanitarian internationalism and democratic nationalism which had been the emotional thread of our intellectuals' life. We had suddenly to make a new orientation. There were mental conflicts. Our latent colonialism strove with our longing for American unity. Our desire for peace strove with our desire for national responsibility in the world. That first lofty and remote and not altogether unsound feeling of our spiritual isolation from the conflict could not last. There was the itch to be in the great experience which the rest of the world was having. Numbers of intelligent people who had never been stirred by the horrors of capitalistic peace at home were shaken out of their slumber by the horrors of war in Belgium. Never having felt responsibility for labor wars and oppressed masses and excluded races at home, they had a large fund of idle emotional capital to invest in the oppressed nationalities and ravaged villages of Europe. Hearts that had felt only ugly contempt for democratic strivings at home beat in tune with the struggle for freedom abroad. All this was natural, but it tended to over-emphasize our responsibility. And it threw our thinking out of gear. The task of making our own country detailedly fit for peace was abandoned in favor of a feverish concern for the management of the war, advice to the fighting governments on all matters, military, social and political, and a gradual working up of the conviction that we were ordained as a nation to lead all erring brothers towards the light of liberty and democracy. The failure of the American intellectual class to erect a creative attitude toward the war can be explained by these sterile mental conflicts which the shock to our ideals sent raging through us.

Mental conflicts end either in a new and higher synthesis or adjustment, or else in a reversion to more primitive ideas which have been outgrown but to which we drop when jolted out of our attained position. The war caused in America a recrudescence of nebulous ideals which a younger generation was fast outgrowing because it had passed the wistful stage and was discovering concrete ways of getting them incarnated in actual institutions. The shock of the war threw us back from this pragmatic work into an emotional bath of these old ideals. There was even a somewhat rarefied revival of our primitive Yankee boastfulness, the reversion of senility to that republican childhood when we expected the whole world to copy our republican institutions. We amusingly ignored the fact that it was just that Imperial German régime, to whom we are to teach the art of self-government, which our own Federal structure, with its executive irresponsible in foreign policy and with its absence of parliamentary control, most resembles. And we are missing the exquisite irony of the unaffected homage paid by the American democratic intellectuals to the last and most detested of Britain's tory premiers as the representative of a "liberal" ally, as well as the irony of the selection

216

of the best hated of America's bourbon "old guard" as the missionary of American democracy to Russia.

The intellectual state that could produce such things is one where reversion has taken place to more primitive ways of thinking. Simple syllogisms are substituted for analysis, things are known by their labels, our heart's desire dictates what we shall see. The American intellectual class, having failed to make the higher syntheses, regresses to ideas that can issue in quick, simplified action. Thought becomes any easy rationalization of what is actually going on or what is to happen inevitably to-morrow. It is true that certain groups did rationalize their colonialism and attach the doctrine of the inviolability of British sea-power to the doctrine of a League of Peace. But this agile resolution of the mental conflict did not become a higher synthesis, to be creatively developed. It gradually merged into a justification for our going to war. It petrified into a dogma to be propagated. Criticism flagged and emotional propaganda began. Most of the socialists, the college professors and the practitioners of literature, however, have not even reached this high-water mark of synthesis. Their mental conflicts have been resolved much more simply. War in the interests of democracy! This was almost the sum of their philosophy. The primitive idea to which they regressed became almost insensibly translated into a craving for action. War was seen as the crowning relief of their indecision. At last action, irresponsibility, the end of anxious and torturing attempts to reconcile peace-ideals with the drag of the world towards Hell.

An end to the pain of trying to adjust the facts to what they ought to be! Let us consecrate the facts as ideal! Let us join the greased slide towards war! The momentum increased. Hesitations, ironies, consciences, considerations,—all were drowned in the elemental blare of doing something aggressive, colossal. The new-found Sabbath "peacefulness of being at war"! The thankfulness with which so many intellectuals lay down and floated with the current betrays the hesitation and suspense through which they had been. The American university is a brisk and happy place these days. Simple, unquestioning action has superseded the knots of thought. The thinker dances with reality.

With how many of the acceptors of war has it been mostly a dread of intellectual suspense? It is a mistake to suppose that intellectuality necessarily makes for suspended judgments. The intellect craves certitude. It takes effort to keep it supple and pliable. In a time of danger and disaster we jump desperately for some dogma to cling to. The time comes, if we try to hold out, when our nerves are sick with fatigue, and we seize in a great healing wave of release some doctrine that can be immediately translated into action. Neutrality meant suspense, and so it became the object of loathing to frayed nerves. The vital myth of the League of Peace provides a dogma to jump to. With war the world becomes motor again and speculation is brushed aside like cobwebs. The blessed emotion of self-defense intervenes too, which focused millions in Europe. A few keep up a critical pose after war is begun, but since they usually advise action which is in one-to-one correspondence with what the mass is already doing, their criticism is little more than a rationalization of the common emotional drive.

The results of war on the intellectual class are already apparent. Their thought becomes little more than a description and justification of what is going on. They turn upon any rash one who continues idly to speculate. Once the war is on, the conviction spreads that individual thought is helpless, that the only way one can count is as a cog in the great wheel. There is no good holding back. We are told to dry our unnoticed and ineffective tears and plunge into the great work. Not only is every one forced into line, but the new certitude becomes idealized. It is a noble realism which opposes itself to futile obstruction and the cowardly refusal to face facts. This realistic boast is so loud and sonorous that one wonders whether realism is always a stern and intelligent grappling with realities. May it not be sometimes a mere surrender to the actual, an abdication of the ideal through a sheer fatigue from intellectual suspense? The pacifist is roundly scolded for refusing to face the facts, and for retiring into his own world of sentimental desire. But is the realist, who refuses to challenge or criticize facts, entitled to any more credit than that which comes from following the line of least resistance? The realist thinks he at least can control events by linking himself to the forces that are moving. Perhaps he can. But if it is a question of controlling war, it is difficult to see how the child on the back of a mad elephant is to be any more effective in stopping the beast than is the child who tries to stop him from the ground. The ex-humanitarian, turned realist, sneers at the snobbish neutrality, colossal conceit, crooked thinking, dazed sensibilities, of those who are still unable to find any balm of consolation for this war. We manufacture consolations here in America while there are probably not a dozen men fighting in Europe who did not long ago give up every reason for their being there except that nobody knew how to get them away.

But the intellectuals whom the crisis has crystallized into an acceptance of war have put themselves into a terrifyingly strategic position. It is only on the craft, in the stream, they say, that one has any chance of controlling the current forces for liberal purposes. If we obstruct, we surrender all power for influence. If we responsibly approve, we then retain our power for guiding. We will be listened to as responsible thinkers, while those who obstructed the coming of war have committed intellectual suicide and shall be cast into outer darkness. Criticism by the ruling powers will only be accepted from those intellectuals who are in sympathy with the general tendency of the war. Well, it is true that they may guide, but if their stream leads to disaster and the frustration of national life, is their guiding any more than a preference whether they shall go over the right-hand or the left-hand side of the precipice? Meanwhile, however, there is comfort on board. Be with us, they call, or be negligible, irrelevant. Dissenters are already excommunicated. Irreconcilable radicals, wringing their hands among the débris, become the most despicable and impotent of men. There seems no choice for the intellectual but to join the mass of acceptance. But again the terrible dilemma arises, —either support what is going on, in which case you count for nothing because you are swallowed in the mass and great incalculable forces bear you on; or remain aloof, passively resistant, in which case you count for nothing because you are outside the machinery of reality.

Is there no place left, then, for the intellectual who cannot yet crystallize, who does not dread suspense, and is not yet drugged with fatigue? The American intellectuals, in their preoccupation with reality, seem to have forgotten that the real enemy is War rather than imperial Germany. There is work to be done to prevent this war of ours from passing into popular mythology as a holy crusade. What shall we do with leaders who tell us that we go to war in moral spotlessness, or who make "democracy" synonymous with a republican form of government? There is work to be done in still shouting that all the revolutionary by-products will not justify the war, or make war anything else than the most noxious complex of all the evils that afflict men. There must be some to find no consolation whatever, and some to sneer at those who buy the cheap emotion of sacrifice. There must be some irreconcilables left who will not even accept the war with walrus tears. There must be some to call unceasingly for peace, and some to insist that the terms of settlement shall be not only liberal but democratic. There must be some intellectuals who are not willing to use the old discredited counters again and to support a peace which would leave all the old inflammable materials of armament lying about the world. There must still be opposition to any contemplated "liberal" world-order founded on military coalitions. The "irreconcilable" need not be disloyal. He need not even be "impossibilist." His apathy towards war should take the form of a heightened energy and enthusiasm for the education, the art, the interpretation that make for life in the midst of the world of death. The intellectual who retains his animus against war will push out more boldly than ever to make his case solid against it. The old ideals crumble; new ideals must be forged. His mind will continue to roam widely and ceaselessly. The thing he will fear most is premature crystallization. If the American intellectual class rivets itself to a "liberal" philosophy that perpetuates the old errors, there will then be need for "democrats" whose task will be to divide, confuse, disturb, keep the intellectual waters constantly in motion to prevent any such ice from ever forming.

A War Diary

September, 1917

TIME BRINGS A BETTER adjustment to the war. There had been so many times when, to those who had energetically resisted its coming, it seemed the last intolerable outrage. In one's wilder moments one expected revolt against the impressment of unwilling men and the suppression of unorthodox opinion. One conceived the war as breaking down through a kind of intellectual sabotage diffused through the country. But as one talks to people outside the cities and away from ruling currents of opinion, one finds the prevailing apathy shot everywhere with acquiescence. The war is a bad business, which somehow got fastened on us. They don't want to go, but they've got to go. One decides that nothing generally obstructive is going to happen and that it would make little difference if it did. The kind of war which we are conducting is an enterprise which the American government does not have to carry on with the hearty coöperation of the American people but only with their acquiescence. And that acquiescence seems sufficient to float an indefinitely protracted war for vague or even largely uncomprehended and unaccepted purposes. Our resources in men and materials are vast enough to organize the war-technique without enlisting more than a fraction of the people's conscious energy. Many men will not like being sucked into the actual fighting organism, but as the war goes on they will be sucked in as individuals and they will yield. There is likely to be no element in the country with the effective will to help them resist. They are not likely to resist of themselves concertedly. They will be licked grudgingly into military shape, and their lack of enthusiasm will in no way unfit them for use in the hecatombs necessary for the military decision upon which Allied political wisdom still apparently insists. It is unlikely that enough men will be taken from the potentially revolting classes seriously to embitter their spirit. Losses in the well-to-do classes will be sustained by a sense of duty and of reputable sacrifice. From the point of view of the worker, it will make little difference whether his work contributes to annihilation overseas or to construction at home. Temporarily, his condition is better if it contributes to the former. We of the middle classes will be progressively poorer than we should otherwise have been. Our lives will be slowly drained by clumsily levied taxes and the robberies of imperfectly controlled private enterprises. But this will not cause us to revolt. There are not likely to be enough hungry stomachs to make a revolution. The materials seem generally absent from the country, and as long as a government wants to use the war-technique in its realization of great ideas, it can count serenely on the human resources of the country, regardless of popular mandate or understanding.

II

If human resources are fairly malleable into the war-technique, our material resources will prove to be even more so, quite regardless of the individual patriotism of their owners or workers. It is almost purely a problem of diversion. Factories and mines and farms will continue to turn out the same products and at an intensified rate, but the government will be working to use their activity and concentrate it as contributory to the war. The process which the piping times of benevolent neutrality began will be pursued to its extreme end. All this will be successful, however, precisely as it is made a matter of centralized governmental organization and not of individual offerings of goodwill and enterprise. It will be coercion from above that will do the trick rather than patriotism from below. Democratic contentment may be shed over the land for a time through the appeal to individual thoughtfulness in saving and in relinquishing profits. But all that is really needed is the coöperation with government of the men who direct the large financial and industrial enterprises. If their interest is enlisted in diverting the mechanism of production into war-channels, it makes not the least difference whether you or I want our activity to count in aid of the war. Whatever we do will contribute toward its successful organization, and toward the riveting of a semi-military State-socialism on the country. As long as the effective managers, the "big men" in the staple industries remained loyal, nobody need care what the millions of little human cogs who had to earn their living felt or thought. This is why the technical organization for this American war goes on so much more rapidly than any corresponding popular sentiment for its aims and purposes. Our war is teaching us that patriotism is really a superfluous quality in war. The government of a modern organized plutocracy does not have to ask whether the people want to fight or understand what they are fighting for, but only whether they will tolerate fighting. America does not coöperate with the President's designs. She rather feebly acquiesces. But that feeble acquiescence is the all-important factor. We are learning that war doesn't need enthusiasm, doesn't need conviction, doesn't need hope, to sustain it. Once maneuvered, it takes care of itself, provided only that our industrial rulers see that the end of the war will leave American capital in a strategic position for world-enterprise. The American people might be much more indifferent to the war even than they are and yet the results would not be materially different. A majority of them might even be feebly or at least unconcertedly hostile to the war, and yet it would go gaily on. That is why a popular referendum seems so supremely irrelevant to people who are

226

willing to use war as an instrument in the working-out of national policy. And that is why this war, with apathy rampant, is probably going to act just as if every person in the country were filled with patriotic ardor, and furnished with a completely assimilated map of the League to Enforce Peace. If it doesn't, the cause will not be the lack of popular ardor, but the clumsiness of the government officials in organizing the technique of the war. Our country in war, given efficiency at the top, can do very well without our patriotism. The non-patriotic man need feel no pangs of conscience about not helping the war. Patriotism fades into the merest trivial sentimentality when it becomes, as so obviously in a situation like this, so pragmatically impotent. As long as one has to earn one's living or buy tax-ridden goods, one is making one's contribution to war in a thousand indirect ways. The war, since it does not need it, cannot fairly demand also the sacrifice of one's spiritual integrity.

III

The "liberals" who claim a realistic and pragmatic attitude in politics have disappointed us in setting up and then clinging wistfully to the belief that our war could get itself justified for an idealistic flavor, or at least for a world-renovating social purpose, that they had more or less denied to the other belligerents. If these realists had

had time in the hurry and scuffle of events to turn their philosophy on themselves, they might have seen how thinly disguised a rationalization this was of their emotional undertow. They wanted a League of Nations. They had an unanalyzable feeling that this was a war in which we had to be, and be in it we would. What more natural than to join the two ideas and conceive our war as the decisive factor in the attainment of the desired end! This gave them a good conscience for willing American participation, although as good men they must have loathed war and everything connected with it. The realist cannot deny facts. Moreover, he must not only acknowledge them but he must use them. Good or bad, they must be turned by his intelligence to some constructive end. Working along with the materials which events give him, he must get where and what he can, and bring something brighter and better out of the chaos.

Now war is such an indefeasible and unescapable Real that the good realist must accept it rather comprehensively. To keep out of it is pure quietism, an acute moral failure to adjust. At the same time, there is an inexorability about war. It is a little unbridled for the realist's rather nice sense of purposive social control. And nothing is so disagreeable to the pragmatic mind as any kind of an absolute. The realistic pragmatist could not recognize war as inexorable—though to the common mind it would seem as near an absolute, coercive social situation as it is possible to fall into. For the inexorable abolishes choices, and it is the essence of the realist's creed to have, in every situation, alternatives before him. He gets out of his scrape in this way: Let the inexorable roll in upon me, since it must. But then, keeping firm my sense of control, I will somehow tame it and turn it to my own creative purposes. Thus realism is justified of her children, and the "liberal" is saved from the limbo of the wailing and irreconcilable pacifists who could not make so easy an adjustment.

Thus the "liberals" who made our war their own preserved their pragmatism. But events have shown how fearfully they imperilled their intuition and how untameable an inexorable really is. For those of us who knew a real inexorable when we saw one, and had learned from watching war what follows the loosing of a war-technique, foresaw how quickly aims and purposes would be forgotten, and how flimsy would be any liberal control of events. It is only we now who can appreciate *The New Republic*—the organ of applied pragmatic realism—when it complains that the League of Peace (which we entered the war to guarantee) is more remote than it was eight months ago; or that our State Department has no diplomatic policy (though it was to realize the high aims of the President's speeches that the intellectuals willed American participation); or that we are subordinating the political management of the war to real or supposed military advantages, (though militarism in the liberal mind had no justification except as a tool for advanced social ends). If after all the idealism and creative intelligence that were shed upon America's taking up of arms, our State Department has no policy, we are like brave passengers who have set out for the Isles of the Blest only to find that the first mate has gone insane and jumped overboard, the rudder has come loose and dropped to the bottom of the sea, and the captain and pilot are lying dead drunk under the wheel. The stokers and engineers, however, are still merrily forcing the speed up to twenty knots an hour and the passengers are presumably getting the pleasure of the ride.

IV

The penalty the realist pays for accepting war is to see disappear one by one the justifications for accepting it. He must either become a genuine Realpolitiker and brazen it through, or else he must feel sorry for his intuition and regretful that he willed the war. But so easy is forgetting and so slow the change of events that he is more likely to ignore the collapse of his case. If he finds that his government is relinquishing the crucial moves of that strategy for which he was willing to use the technique of war, he is likely to move easily to the ground that it will all come out in the end the same anyway. He soon becomes satisfied with tacitly ratifying whatever happens, or at least straining to find the grain of unplausible hope that may be latent in the situation.

But what then is there really to choose between the realist who accepts evil in order to manipulate it to a great end, but who somehow unaccountably finds events turn sour on him and the Utopian pacifist who cannot stomach the evil and will have none of it? Both are helpless, both are coerced. The Utopian, however, knows that he is ineffective and that he is coerced, while the realist, evading disillusionment, moves in a twilight zone of half-hearted criticism, and hopings for the best, where he does not become a tacit fatalist. The latter would be the manlier position, but then where would be his realistic philosophy of intelligence and choice? Professor Dewey has become impatient at the merely good and merely conscientious objectors to war who do not attach their conscience and intelligence to forces moving in another direction. But in wartime there are literally no valid forces moving in another direction. War determines its own end—victory, and government crushes out automatically all forces that deflect, or threaten to deflect, energy from the path of organization to that end. All governments will act in this way, the most democratic as well as the most autocratic. It is only "liberal" naïveté that is shocked at arbitrary coercion and suppression. Willing war means willing all the evils that are organically bound up with it. A good many people still seem to believe in a peculiar kind of democratic and antiseptic war. The pacifists opposed the war because they knew this was an illusion, and because of the myriad hurts they knew war would do the promise of democracy at home. For once the babes and sucklings seem to have been wiser than the children of light.

V

If it is true that the war will go on anyway whether it is popular or not or whether its purposes are clear, and if it is true that in wartime constructive realism is an illusion, then the aloof man, the man who will not obstruct the war but who cannot spiritually accept it, has a clear case for himself. Our war presents no more extraordinary phenomenon than the number of the more creative minds of the younger generation who are still irreconcilable toward the great national enterprise which the government has undertaken. The country is still dotted with young men and women, in full possession of their minds, faculties and virtue, who feel themselves profoundly alien to the work which is going on around them. They must not be confused with the disloyal or the pro-German. They have no grudge against the country, but their patriotism has broken down in the emergency. They want to see the carnage stopped and Europe decently constructed again. They want a democratic peace. If the swift crushing of Germany will bring that peace, they want to see Germany crushed. If the embargo on neutrals will prove the decisive coup, they are willing to see the neutrals taken ruthlessly by the throat. But they do not really believe that peace will come by any of these means, or by any use of our war-technique whatever. They are genuine pragmatists and they fear any kind of an absolute, even when bearing gifts. They know that the longer a war lasts the harder it is to make peace. They know that the peace of exhaustion is a dastardly peace, leaving enfeebled the morale of the defeated, and leaving invincible for years all the most greedy and soulless elements in the conquerors. They feel that the greatest obstacle to peace now is the lack of the powerful mediating neutral which we might have been. They see that war has lost for us both the mediation and the leadership, and is blackening us ever deeper with the responsibility for having prolonged the dreadful tangle. They are skeptical not only of the technique of war, but also of its professed aims. The President's idealism stops just short of the pitch that would arouse their own. There is a middle-aged and belated taint about the best ideals which publicist liberalism has been able to express. The appeals to propagate political democracy leave these people cold in a world which has become so disillusioned of democracy in the face of universal economic servitude. Their ideals outshoot the government's. To them the real arena lies in the international class-struggle, rather than in the competition of artificial national units. They are watching to see what the Russian socialists are going to do for the world, not what the timorous capitalistic American democracy may be planning. They can feel no enthusiasm for a League of Nations, which should solidify the old units and continue in disguise the old theories of international relations. Indispensable, perhaps? But not inspiring; not something to give one's spiritual allegiance to. And yet the best advice that American wisdom can offer to those who are out of sympathy with the war is to turn one's influence toward securing that our war contribute toward this end. But why would not this League turn out to be little more than a well-oiled machine for the use of that enlightened imperialism toward which liberal American finance is already whetting its tongue? And what is enlightened imperialism as an international ideal as against the anarchistic communism of the nations which the new Russia suggests in renouncing imperialist intentions?

VI

Skeptical of the means and skeptical of the aims, this element of the younger generation stands outside the war, and looks upon the conscript army and all the other war-activities as troublesome interruptions on its thought and idealism, interruptions which do not touch anywhere a fiber of its soul. Some have been much more disturbed than others, because of the determined challenge of both patriots and realists to break in with the war-obsession which has filled for them their sky. Patriots and realists can both be answered. They must not be allowed to shake one's inflexible determination not to be spiritually implicated in the war. It is foolish to hope. Since the 30th of July, 1914, nothing has happened in the arena of war-policy and war-technique except for the complete and unmitigated worst. We are tired of continued disillusionment, and of the betrayal of generous anticipations. It is saner not to waste energy in hope within the system of war-enterprise. One may accept dispassionately whatever changes for good may happen from the war, but one will not allow one's imagination to connect them organically with war. It is better to resist cheap consolations, and remain skeptical about any of the good things so confidently promised us either through victory or the social reorganization demanded by the war-technique. One keeps healthy in wartime not by a series of religious and political consolations that something good is coming out of it all, but by a vigorous assertion of values in which war has no part. Our skepticism can be made a shelter behind which is built up a wider consciousness of the personal and social and artistic ideals which American civilization needs to lead the good life. We can be skeptical constructively, if, thrown back on our inner resources from the world of war which is taken as the overmastering reality, we search much more actively to clarify our attitudes and express a richer significance in the American scene. We do not feel the war to be very real, and we sense a singular air of falsity about the emotions of the upper-classes toward everything connected with war. This ostentatious shame, this groveling before illusory Allied heroisms and nobilities, has shocked us. Minor novelists and minor poets and minor publicists are still coming back from driving ambulances in France to write books that nag us into an appreciation of the "real meaning." No one can object to the generous emotions of service in a great cause or to the horror and pity at colossal devastation and agony. But too many of these prophets are men who have lived rather briskly among the cruelties and thinnesses of American civilization and have shown no obvious horror and pity at the exploitations and the arid quality of the life lived here around us. Their moral sense had been deeply stirred by what they saw in France and Belgium, but it was a moral sense relatively unpracticed by deep concern and reflection over the inadequacies of American democracy. Few of them had used their vision to create literature impelling us toward a more radiant American future. And that is why, in spite of their vivid stirrings, they seem so unconvincing. Their idealism is too new and bright to affect us, for it comes from men who never cared very particularly about great creative American ideas. So these writers come to us less like ardent youth, pouring its energy into the great causes, than like youthful mouthpieces of their strident and belligerent elders. They did not convert us, but rather drove us farther back into the rightness of American isolation.

VII

There was something incredibly mean and plebeian about that abasement into which the war-partisans tried to throw us all. When we were urged to squander our emotion on a bedeviled Europe, our intuition told us how much all rich and generous emotions were needed at home to leaven American civilization. If we refused to export them it was because we wanted to see them at work here. It is true that great reaches of American prosperous life were not using generous emotions for any purpose whatever. But the real antithesis was not between being concerned about luxurious automobiles and being concerned about the saving of France. America's "benevolent neutrality" had been saving the Allies for three years through the ordinary channels of industry and trade. We could afford to export material goods and credit far more than we could afford to export emotional capital. The real antithesis was between interest in expensively exploiting American material life and interest in creatively enhancing American personal and artistic life. The fat and earthy American could be blamed not for not palpitating more richly about France, but for not palpitating more richly about America and her spiritual drouths. The war will leave the country spiritually impoverished, because of the draining away of sentiment into the channels of war. Creative and constructive enterprises will suffer not only through the appalling waste of financial capital in the work of annihilation, but also in the loss of emotional capital in the conviction that war overshadows all other realities. This is the poison of war that disturbs even creative minds. Writers tell us that, after contact with the war, literature seems an idle pastime, if not an offense, in a world of great deeds. Perhaps literature that can be paled by war will not be missed. We may feel vastly relieved at our salvation from so many feeble novels and graceful verses that khaki-clad authors might have given us. But this nobly-sounding sense of the futility of art in a world of war may easily infect conscientious minds. And it is against this infection that we must fight.

VIII

The conservation of American promise is the present task for this generation of malcontents and aloof men and women. If America has lost its political isolation, it is all the more obligated to retain its spiritual integrity. This does not mean any smug retreat from the world, with a belief that the truth is in us and can only be contaminated by contact. It means that the promise of American life is not yet achieved, perhaps not even seen, and that, until it is, there is nothing for us but stern and intensive cultivation of our garden. Our insulation will not be against any great creative ideas or forms that Europe brings. It will be a turning within in order that we may have something to give without. The old American ideas which are still expected to bring life to the world seem stale and archaic. It is grotesque to try to carry democracy to Russia. It is absurd to try to contribute to the world's store of great moving ideas until we have a culture to give. It is absurd for us to think of ourselves as blessing the world with anything unless we hold it much more self-consciously and significantly than we hold anything now. Mere negative freedom will not do as a twentieth-century principle. American ideas must be dynamic or we are presumptuous in offering them to the world.

IX

The war—or American promise: one must choose. One cannot be interested in both. For the effect of the war will be to impoverish American promise. It cannot advance it, however liberals may choose to identify American promise with a league of nations to enforce peace. Americans who desire to cultivate the promises of American life need not lift a finger to obstruct the war, but they cannot conscientiously accept it. However intimately a part of their country they may feel in its creative enterprises toward a better life, they cannot feel themselves a part of it in its futile and self-mutilating enterprise of war. We can be apathetic with a good conscience, for we have other values and ideals for America. Our country will not suffer for our lack of patriotism as long as it has that of our industrial masters. Meanwhile, those who have turned their thinking into war-channels have abdicated their leadership for this younger generation. They have put themselves in a limbo of interests that are not the concerns which worry us about American life and make us feverish and discontented.

Let us compel the war to break in on us, if it must, not

239

go hospitably to meet it. Let us force it perceptibly to batter in our spiritual walls. This attitude need not be a fatuous hiding in the sand, denying realities. When we are broken in on, we can yield to the inexorable. Those who are conscripted will have been broken in on. If they do not want to be martyrs, they will have to be victims. They are entitled to whatever alleviations are possible in an inexorable world. But the others can certainly resist the attitude that blackens the whole conscious sky with war. They can resist the poison which makes art and all the desires for more impassioned living seem idle and even shameful. For many of us, resentment against the war has meant a vivider consciousness of what we are seeking in American life.

This search has been threatened by two classes who have wanted to deflect idealism to the war,—the patriots and the realists. The patriots have challenged us by identifying apathy with disloyalty. The reply is that wartechnique in this situation is a matter of national mechanics rather than national ardor. The realists have challenged us by insisting that the war is an instrument in the working-out of beneficent national policy. Our skepticism points out to them how soon their "mastery" becomes "drift," tangled in the fatal drive toward victory as its own end, how soon they become mere agents and expositors of forces as they are. Patriots and realists disposed of, we can pursue creative skepticism with honesty, and at least a hope that in the recoil from war we may find the treasures we are looking for.

Twilight of Idols

October, 1917

WHERE ARE THE SEEDS of American promise? Man cannot live by politics alone, and it is small cheer that our best intellects are caught in the political current and see only the hope that America will find her soul in the re-making of the world. If William James were alive would he be accepting the war-situation so easily and compla-cently? Would he be chiding the over-stimulated intelli-gence of peace-loving idealists, and excommunicating from the ranks of liberal progress the pitiful remnant of those who struggle "above the battle"? I like to think that his gallant spirit would have called for a war to be gal-lantly played, with insistent care for democratic values at home, and unequivocal alliance with democratic ele-ments abroad for a peace that should promise more than a mere union of benevolent imperialisms. I think of James now because the recent articles of John Dewey's on the war suggest a slackening in his thought for our guidance and stir, and the inadequacy of his pragmatism as a philos-ophy of life in this emergency. Whether James would have given us just that note of spiritual adventure which would make the national enterprise seem creative for an American future,—this we can never know. But surely that philosophy of Dewey's which we had been following so uncritically for so long, breaks down almost noisily when it is used to grind out interpretation for the present crisis. These articles on "Conscience and Compulsion," "The Future of Pacifism," "What America Will Fight For," "Conscription of Thought," which *The New Republic* has been printing, seem to me to be a little off-color. A philosopher who senses so little the sinister forces of war, who is so much more concerned over the excesses of the pacifists than over the excesses of military policy, who can feel only amusement at the idea that any one should try to conscript thought, who assumes that the war-technique can be used without trailing along with it the mob-fanaticisms, the injustices and hatreds, that are organically bound up with it, is speaking to another element of the younger intelligentsia than that to which I belong. Evidently the attitudes which war calls out are fiercer and more incalculable than Professor Dewey is accustomed to take into his hopeful and intelligent imagination, and the pragmatist mind, in trying to adjust itself to them, gives the air of grappling, like the pioneer who challenges the arid plains, with a power too big for it. It is not an arena of creative intelligence our country's mind is now, but of mob-psychology. The soldiers who tried to lynch Max Eastman showed that current patriotism is not a product of the will to remake the world. The luxuriant releases of explosive hatred for which peace apparently gives far too little scope cannot be wooed by sweet reasonableness, nor can they be the raw material for the creation of rare liberal political structures. All that can be done is to try to keep your country out of situations where such expressive releases occur. If you have willed the situation, however, or accepted it as inevitable, it is fatuous to protest against the gay debauch of hatred and fear and swagger that must mount and mount, until the heady and virulent poison of war shall have created its own anti-toxin of ruin and disillusionment. To talk as if war were anything else than such a poison is to show that your philosophy has never been confronted with the pathless and the inexorable, and that, only dimly feeling the change, it goes ahead acting as if it had not got out of its depth. Only a lack of practice with a world of human nature so raw-nerved, irrational, uncreative, as an America at war was bound to show itself to be, can account for the singular unsatisfactoriness of these later utterances of Dewey. He did have one moment of hesitation just before the war began, when the war and its external purposes and unifying power seemed the small thing beside that internal adventure which should find our American promise. But that perspective has now disappeared, and one finds Dewey now untainted by skepticism as to our being about a business to which all our idealism should rally. That failure to get guaranties that this country's effort would obligate the Allies to a democratic world-order Dewey blames on the defection of the pacifists, and then somehow manages to get himself into a "we" who "romantically," as he says, forewent this crucial link of our strategy. Does this easy identification of himself with undemocratically controlled foreign policy mean that a country is democratic when it accepts what its government does, or that war has a narcotic effect on the pragmatic mind? For Dewey somehow retains his sense of being in the controlling class, and ignores those anxious questions of democrats who have been his disciples but are now resenters of the war.

What I come to is a sense of suddenly being left in the lurch, of suddenly finding that a philosophy upon which I had relied to carry us through no longer works. I find the contrast between the idea that creative intelligence has free functioning in wartime, and the facts of the inexorable situation, too glaring. The contrast between what liberals ought to be doing and saying if democratic values are to be conserved, and what the real forces are imposing upon them, strikes too sternly on my intellectual senses. I should prefer some philosophy of War as the grim and terrible cleanser to this optimism-haunted mood that continues unweariedly to suggest that all can yet be made to work for good in a mad and half-destroyed world. I wonder if James, in the face of such disaster, would not have abandoned his "moral equivalent of war" for an "immoral equivalent" which, in swift and periodic saturnalia, would have acted as vaccination against the sure pestilence of war.

II

Dewey's philosophy is inspiring enough for a society at peace, prosperous and with a fund of progressive good-will. It is a philosophy of hope, of clear-sighted comprehension of materials and means. Where institutions are at all malleable, it is the only clew for improvement. It is scientific method applied to "uplift." But this careful adaptation of means to desired ends, this experimental working out of control over brute forces and dead matter in the interests of communal life, depends on a store of rationality, and is effective only where there is strong desire for progress. It is precisely the school, the institution to which Dewey's philosophy was first applied, that is of all our institutions the most malleable. And it is the will to educate that has seemed, in these days, among all our social attitudes the most rationally motivated. It was education, and almost education alone, that seemed susceptible to the steady pressure of an "instrumental" philosophy. Intelligence really seemed about to come into conscious control of an institution, and that one the most potent in molding the attitudes needed for a civilized society and the aptitudes needed for the happiness of the individual.

For both our revolutionary conceptions of what education means, and for the intellectual strategy of its approach, this country is immeasurably indebted to the influence of Professor Dewey's philosophy. With these ideas sincerely felt, a rational nation would have chosen education as its national enterprise. Into this it would have thrown its energy though the heavens fell and the earth rocked around it. But the nation did not use its isolation from the conflict to educate itself. It fretted for three years and then let war, not education, be chosen, at the almost unanimous behest of our intellectual class, from motives alien to our cultural needs, and for political ends alien to the happiness of the individual. But nations, of course, are not rational entities, and they act within their most irrational rights when they accept war as the most important thing the nation can do in the face of metaphysical menaces of imperial prestige. What concerns us here is the relative ease with which the pragmatist intellectuals, with Professor Dewey at the head, have moved out their philosophy, bag and baggage, from education to war. So abrupt a change in the direction of the national enterprise, one would have expected to cause more emotion, to demand more apologetics. His optimism may have told Professor Dewey that war would not materially demoralize our growth—would, perhaps, after all, be but an incident in the nation's life—but it is not easy to see how, as we skate toward the bankruptcy of war-billions, there will be resources available for educational enterprise that does not contribute directly to the war-technique. Neither is any passion for growth, for creative mastery, going to flourish among the host of militaristic values and new tastes for power that are springing up like poisonous mushrooms on every hand.

How could the pragmatist mind accept war without more violent protest, without a greater wrench? Either Professor Dewey and his friends felt that the forces were too strong for them, that the war had to be, and it was better to take it up intelligently than to drift blindly in; or else they really expected a gallant war, conducted with jealous regard for democratic values at home and a captivating vision of international democracy as the end of all the toil and pain. If their motive was the first, they would seem to have reduced the scope of possible control of events to the vanishing point. If the war is too strong for you to prevent, how is it going to be weak enough for you to control and mold to your liberal purposes? And if their motive was to shape the war firmly for good, they seem to have seriously miscalculated the fierce urgencies of it. Are they to be content, as the materialization of their hopes, with a doubtful League of Nations and the suppression of the I.W.W.? Yet the numbing power of the war-situation seems to have kept them from realizing what has happened to their philosophy. The betrayal of their first hopes has certainly not discouraged them. But neither has it roused them to a more energetic expression of the forces through which they intend to realize them. I search Professor Dewey's articles in vain for clews as to the specific working-out of our democratic desires, either nationally or internationally, either in the present or in the reconstruction after the war. No programme is suggested, nor is there feeling for present vague popular movements and revolts. Rather are the latter chided, for their own vagueness and impracticalities. Similarly, with the other prophets of instrumentalism who accompany Dewey into the war, democracy remains an unanalyzed term, useful as a call to battle, but not an intellectual tool, turning up fresh sod for the changing future. Is it the political democracy of a plutocratic America that we are fighting for, or is it the social democracy of the new Russia? Which do our rulers really fear more, the menace of Imperial Germany, or the liberating influence of a socialist Russia. In the application of their philosophy to politics, our pragmatists are sliding over this crucial question of ends. Dewey says our ends must be intelligently international rather than chauvinistic. But this gets us little distance along our way.

In this difficult time the light that has been in liberals and radicals has become darkness. If radicals spend their time holding conventions to attest their loyalty and stamp out the "enemies within," they do not spend it in breaking intellectual paths, or giving us shining ideas to which we can attach our faith and conscience. The spiritual apathy from which the more naïve of us suffer, and which the others are so busy fighting, arises largely from sheer default of a clear vision that would melt it away. Let the motley crew of ex-socialists, and labor radicals, and liberals and pragmatist philosophers, who have united for the prosecution of the war, present a coherent and convincing democratic programme, and they will no longer be confronted with the skepticism of the conscientious and the impossibilist. But when the emphasis is on technical organization, rather than organization of ideas, on strategy rather than desires, one begins to suspect that no programme is presented because they have none to present. This burrowing into war-technique hides the void where a democratic philosophy should be. Our intellectuals consort with war-boards in order to keep their minds off the question of what the slow masses of the people are really desiring, or toward what the best hope of the country really drives. Similarly the blaze of patriotism on the part of the radicals serves the purpose of concealing the feebleness of their intellectual light.

Is the answer that clear formulation of democratic ends must be postponed until victory in the war is attained? But to make this answer is to surrender the entire case. For the support of the war by radicals, realists, pragmatists, is due—or so they say—to the fact that the war is not only saving the cause of democracy, but is immensely accelerating its progress. Well, what are those gains? How are they to be conserved? What do they lead to? How can we further them? Into what large idea of society do they group? To ignore these questions, and think only of the war-technique and its accompanying devotions, is to undermine the foundations of these people's own faith.

A policy of "win the war first" must be, for the radical, a policy of intellectual suicide. Their support of the war throws upon them the responsibility of showing inch by inch the democratic gains, and of laying out a charter of specific hopes. Otherwise they confess that they are impotent and that the war is submerging their expectations, or that they are not genuinely imaginative and offer little promise for future leadership.

III

It may seem unfair to group Professor Dewey with Mr. Spargo and Mr. Gompers, Mr. A. M. Simons, and the Vigilantes. I do so only because in their acceptance of the war, they are all living out that popular American "instrumental" philosophy which Professor Dewey has formulated in such convincing and fascinating terms. On an infinitely more intelligent plane, he is yet one with them in his confidence that the war is motivated by democratic ends and is being made to serve them. A high mood of confidence and self-righteousness moves them all, a keen sense of control over events that makes them eligible to discipleship under Professor Dewey's philosophy. They are all hostile to impossibilism, to apathy, to any attitude that is not a cheerful and brisk setting to work to use the emergency to consolidate the gains of democracy. Not, Is it being used? but, Let us make a flutter about using it! This unanimity of mood puts the resenter of war out of the arena. But he can still seek to explain why this philosophy which has no place for the inexorable should have adjusted itself so easily to the inexorable of war, and why, although a philosophy of the creative intelligence in using means toward ends, it should show itself so singularly impoverished in its present supply of democratic values.

What is the matter with the philosophy? One has a sense of having come to a sudden, short stop at the end of an intellectual era. In the crisis, this philosophy of intelligent control just does not measure up to our needs. What is the root of this inadequacy that is felt so keenly by our restless minds? Van Wyck Brooks has pointed out searchingly the lack of poetic vision in our pragmatist "awakeners." Is there something in these realistic attitudes that works actually against poetic vision, against concern for the quality of life as above machinery of life? Apparently there is. The war has revealed a younger intelligentsia, trained up in the pragmatic dispensation, immensely ready for the executive ordering of events, pitifully unprepared for the intellectual interpretation or the idealistic focusing of ends. The young men in Belgium, the officers' training corps, the young men being sucked into the councils at Washington and into war-organization everywhere, have among them a definite element, upon whom Dewey, as veteran philosopher, might well bestow a papal blessing. They have absorbed the secret of scientific method as applied to political administration. They are liberal, enlightened, aware. They are touched with creative intelligence toward the solution of political and industrial problems. They are a wholly new force in American life, the product of the swing in the colleges from a training that emphasized classical studies to one that emphasized political and economic values. Practically all this element, one would say, is lined up in service of the war-technique. There seems to have been a peculiar congeniality between the war and these men. It is as if the war and they had been waiting for each other. One wonders what scope they would have had for their intelligence without it. Probably most of them would have gone into industry and devoted themselves to sane reorganization schemes. What is significant is that it is the technical side of the war that appeals to them, not the interpretative or political side. The formulation of values and ideals, the production of articulate and suggestive thinking, had not, in their education, kept pace, to any extent whatever, with their technical aptitude. The result is that the field of intellectual formulation is very poorly manned by this younger intelligentsia. While they organize the war, formulation of opinion is left largely in the hands of professional patriots, sensational editors, archaic radicals. The intellectual work of this younger intelligentsia is done by the sedition-hunting Vigilantes, and by the saving remnant of older liberals. It is true, Dewey calls for a more attentive formulation of war-purposes and ideas, but he calls largely to deaf ears. His disciples have learned all too literally the instrumental attitude toward life, and, being immensely intelligent and energetic, they are making themselves efficient instruments of the war-technique, accepting with little question the ends as announced from above. That those ends are largely negative does not concern them, because they have never learned not to subordinate idea to technique. Their education has not given them a coherent system of large ideas, or a feeling for democratic goals. They have, in short, no clear philosophy of life except that of intelligent service, the admirable adaptation of means to ends. They are vague as to what kind of a society they want, or what kind of society America needs, but they are equipped with all the administrative attitudes and talents necessary to attain it.

To those of us who have taken Dewey's philosophy almost as our American religion, it never occurred that values could be subordinated to technique. We were instrumentalists, but we had our private utopias so clearly before our minds that the means fell always into its place as contributory. And Dewey, of course, always meant his philosophy, when taken as a philosophy of life, to start with values. But there was always that unhappy ambiguity in his doctrine as to just how values were created, and it became easier and easier to assume that just any growth was justified and almost any activity valuable so long as it achieved ends. The American, in living out this philosophy, has habitually confused results with product, and been content with getting somewhere without asking too closely whether it was the desirable place to get. It is now becoming plain that unless you start with the vividest kind of poetic vision, your instrumentalism is likely to land you just where it has landed this younger intelligentsia which is so happily and busily engaged in the national enterprise of war. You must have your vision and you must have your technique. The practical effect of Dewey's philosophy has evidently been to develop the sense of the latter at the expense of the former. Though he himself would develop them together, even in him there seems to be a flagging of values, under the influence of war. *The New Republic* honorably clamors for the Allies to subordinate military strategy to political ends, technique to democratic values. But war always undermines values. It is the outstanding lesson of the whole war that statesmen cannot be trusted to get this perspective right, that their only motto is, first to win and then grab what they can. The struggle against this statesmanlike animus must be a losing one as long as we have not very clear and very determined and very revolutionary democratic ideas and programmes to challenge them with. The trouble with our situation is not only that values have been generally ignored in favor of technique, but that those who have struggled to keep values foremost, have been too bloodless and too nearsighted in their vision. The defect of any philosophy of "adaptation" or "adjustment," even when it means adjustment to changing, living experience, is that there is no provision for thought or experience getting beyond itself. If your ideal is to be adjustment to your situation, in radiant co-operation with reality, then your success is likely to be just that and no more. You never transcend anything.

You grow, but your spirit never jumps out of your skin to go on wild adventures. If your policy as a publicist reformer is to take what you can get, you are likely to find that you get something less than you should be willing to take. Italy in the settlement is said to be demanding one hundred in order to get twenty, and this Machiavellian principle might well be adopted by the radical. Vision must constantly outshoot technique, opportunist efforts usually achieve less even than what seemed obviously possible. An impossibilist élan that appeals to desire will often carry further. A philosophy of adjustment will not even make for adjustment. If you try merely to "meet" situations as they come, you will not even meet them. Instead you will only pile up behind you deficits and arrears that will some day bankrupt you.

We are in the war because an American government practiced a philosophy of adjustment, and an instrumentalism for minor ends, instead of creating new values and setting at once a large standard to which the nations might repair. An intellectual attitude of mere adjustment, of mere use of the creative intelligence to make your progress, must end in caution, regression, and a virtual failure to effect even that change which you so clear-sightedly and desirously see. This is the root of our dissatisfaction with much of the current political and social realism that is preached to us. It has everything good and wise except the obstreperous vision that would drive and draw all men into it.

IV

The working-out of this American philosophy in our intellectual life then has meant an exaggerated emphasis on the mechanics of life at the expense of the quality of living. We suffer from a real shortage of spiritual values. A philosophy that worked when we were trying to get that material foundation for American life in which more impassioned living could flourish no longer works when we are faced with inexorable disaster and the hysterias of the mob. The note of complacency which we detect in the current expressions of this philosophy has a bad taste. The congruous note for the situation would seem to be, on the contrary, that of robust desperation,—a desperation that shall rage and struggle until new values come out of the travail, and we see some glimmering of our democratic way. In the creation of these new values, we may expect the old philosophy, the old radicalism, to be helpless. It has found a perfectly definite level, and there is no reason to think that it will not remain there. Its flowering appears in the technical organization of the war by an earnest group of young liberals, who direct their course by an opportunist programme of State-socialism at home and a league of benevolently imperialistic nations abroad. At their best they can give us a government by prudent, enlightened college men instead of by politicians. At their best, they can abolish war by making everybody a partner in the booty of exploitation. That is all, and it is technically admirable. Only there is nothing in the outlook that touches in any way the happiness of the individual, the vivifying of the personality, the comprehension of social forces, the flair of art,—in other words, the quality of life. Our intellectuals have failed us as value-creators, even as value-emphasizers. The allure of the martial in war has passed only to be succeeded by the allure of the technical. The allure of fresh and true ideas, of free speculation, of artistic vigor, of cultural styles, of intelligence suffused by feeling, and feeling given fiber and outline by intelligence, has not come, and can hardly come, we see now, while our reigning philosophy is an instrumental one.

Whence can come this allure? Only from those who are thorough malcontents. Irritation at things as they are, disgust at the continual frustrations and aridities of American life, deep dissatisfaction with self and with the groups that give themselves forth as hopeful,—out of such moods there might be hammered new values. The malcontents would be men and women who could not stomach the war, or the reactionary idealism that has followed in its train. They are quite through with the professional critics and classicists who have let cultural values die through their own personal ineptitude. Yet these malcontents have no intention of being cultural vandals, only to slay. They are not barbarians, but seek the vital and the sincere everywhere. All they want is a new orientation of the spirit that shall be modern, an orientation to accompany that technical orientation which is fast coming, and which the war accelerates. They will be harsh and often bad-tempered, and they will feel that the break-up of things is no time for mellowness. They will have a taste for spiritual adventure, and for sinister imaginative excursions. It will not be Puritanism so much as complacency that they will fight. A tang, a bitterness, an intellectual fiber, a verve, they will look for in literature, and their most virulent enemies will be those unaccountable radicals who are still morally servile, and are now trying to suppress all free speculation in the interests of nationalism. Something more mocking, more irreverent, they will constantly want. They will take institutions very lightly, indeed will never fail to be surprised at the seriousness with which good radicals take the stated offices and systems. Their own contempt will be scarcely veiled, and they will be glad if they can tease, provoke, irritate thought on any subject. These malcontents will be more or less of the American tribe of talent who used either to go immediately to Europe, or starved submissively at home. But these people will neither go to Europe, nor starve submissively. They are too much entangled emotionally in the possibilities of American life to leave it, and they have no desire whatever to starve. So they are likely to go ahead beating their heads at the wall until they are either bloody or light appears. They will give offense to their elders who cannot see what all the concern is about, and they will hurt the more middle-aged sense of adventure upon which the better integrated minds of the younger generation will have compromised. Optimism is often compensatory, and the optimistic mood in American thought may mean merely that American life is too terrible to face. A more skeptical, malicious, desperate, ironical mood may actually be the sign of more vivid and more stirring life fermenting in America to-day. It may be a sign of hope. That thirst for more of the intellectual "war and laughter" that we find Nietzsche calling us to may bring us satisfactions that optimism-haunted philosophies could never bring. Malcontentedness may be the beginning of promise. That is why I evoked the spirit of William James, with its gay passion for ideas, and its freedom of speculation, when I felt the slightly pedestrian gait into which the war had brought pragmatism. It is the creative desire more than the creative intelligence that we shall need if we are ever to fly.

Trans-National America

No REVERBERATORY effect of the great war has caused American public opinion more solicitude than the failure of the "melting-pot." The discovery of diverse nationalistic feelings among our great alien population has come to most people as an intense shock. It has brought out the unpleasant inconsistencies of our traditional beliefs. We have had to watch hard-hearted old Brahmins virtuously indignant at the spectacle of the immigrant refusing to be melted, while they jeer at patriots like Mary Antin who write about "our forefathers." We have had to listen to publicists who express themselves as stunned by the evidence of vigorous nationalistic and cultural movements in this country among Germans, Scandinavians, Bohemians, and Poles, while in the same breath they insist that the alien shall be forcibly assimilated to that Anglo-Saxon tradition which they unquestioningly label "American."

As the unpleasant truth has come upon us that assimilation in this country was proceeding on lines very different from those we had marked out for it, we found ourselves inclined to blame those who were thwarting our prophecies. The truth became culpable. We blamed the war, we blamed the Germans. And then we discovered with a moral shock that these movements had been making great headway before the war even began. We found that the tendency, reprehensible and paradoxical as it might be, has been for the national clusters of immigrants, as they became more and more firmly established and more and more prosperous, to cultivate more and more assiduously the literatures and cultural traditions of their homelands. Assimilation, in other words, instead of washing out the memories of Europe, made them more and more intensely real. Just as these clusters became more and more objectively American, did they become more and more German or Scandinavian or Bohemian or Polish.

To face the fact that our aliens are already strong enough to take a share in the direction of their own destiny, and that the strong cultural movements represented by the foreign press, schools, and colonies are a challenge to our facile attempts, is not, however, to admit the failure of Americanization. It is not to fear the failure of democracy. It is rather to urge us to an investigation of what Americanism may rightly mean. It is to ask ourselves whether our ideal has been broad or narrow—whether perhaps the time has not come to assert a higher ideal than the "melting-pot." Surely we cannot be certain of our spiritual democracy when, claiming to melt the nations within us to a comprehension of our free and democratic institutions, we fly into panic at the first sign of their own will and tendency. We act as if we wanted Americanization to take place only on our own terms, and not by the consent of the governed. All our elaborate machinery of settlement and school and union, of social and political naturalization, however, will move with friction just in so far as it neglects to take into account this strong and virile insistence that America shall be what the immigrant will have a hand in making it, and not what a ruling class, descendant of those British stocks which were the first permanent immigrants, decide that America shall be made. This is the condition which confronts us, and which demands a clear and general readjustment of our attitude and our ideal.

I

Mary Antin is right when she looks upon our foreign-born as the people who missed the Mayflower and came over on the first boat they could find. But she forgets that when they did come it was not upon other Mayflowers, but upon a "Maiblume," a "Fleur de Mai," a "Fior di Maggio," "Majblomst." These people were not mere arrivals from the same family, to be welcomed as understood and long-loved, but strangers to the neighborhood, with whom a long process of settling down had to take place. For they brought with them their national and racial characters, and each new national quota had to wear slowly away the contempt with which its mere alienness got itself greeted. Each had to make its way slowly from the lowest strata of unskilled labor up to a level where it satisfied the accredited norms of social success.

We are all foreign-born or the descendants of foreign-born, and if distinctions are to be made between us they should rightly be on some other ground than indigenousness. The early colonists came over with motives no less colonial than the later. They did not come to be assimilated in an American melting-pot. They did not come to adopt the culture of the American Indian. They had not the smallest intention of "giving themselves without reservation" to the new country. They came to get freedom to live as they wanted to. They came to escape from the stifling air and chaos of the old world; they came to make their fortune in a new land. They invented no new social framework. Rather they brought over bodily the old ways to which they had been accustomed. Tightly concentrated on a hostile frontier, they were conservative beyond belief. Their pioneer daring was reserved for the objective conquest of material resources. In their folkways, in their social and political institutions, they were, like every colonial people, slavishly imitative of the mother-country. So that, in spite of the "Revolution," our whole legal and political system remained more English than the English, petrified and unchanging, while in England itself law developed to meet the needs of the changing times.

It is just this English-American conservatism that has been our chief obstacle to social advance. We have needed the new peoples—the order of the German and Scandina-

263

vian, the turbulence of the Slav and Hun—to save us from our own stagnation. I do not mean that the illiterate Slav is now the equal of the New Englander of pure descent. He is raw material to be educated, not into a New Englander, but into a socialized American along such lines as those thirty nationalities are being educated in the amazing schools of Gary. I do not believe that this process is to be one of decades of evolution. The spectacle of Japan's sudden jump from mediaevalism to post-modernism should have destroyed that superstition. We are not dealing with individuals who are to "evolve." We are dealing with their children, who, with that education we are about to have, will start level with all of us. Let us cease to think of ideals like democracy as magical qualities inherent in certain peoples. Let us speak, not of inferior races, but of inferior civilizations. We are all to educate and to be educated. These peoples in America are in a common enterprise. It is not what we are now that concerns us, but what this plastic next generation may become in the light of a new cosmopolitan ideal.

We are not dealing with static factors, but with fluid and dynamic generations. To contrast the older and the newer immigrants and see the one class as democratically motivated by love of liberty, and the other by mere money-getting, is not to illuminate the future. To think of earlier nationalities as culturally assimilated to America, while we picture the later as a sodden and resistive mass, makes only for bitterness and misunderstanding. There may be a difference between these earlier and these later stocks, but it lies neither in motive for coming nor in strength of cultural allegiance to the homeland. The truth is that no more tenacious cultural allegiance to the mother country has been shown by any alien nation than by the ruling class of Anglo-Saxon descendants in these American States. English snobberies, English religion, English literary styles, English literary reverences and canons, English ethics, English superiorities, have been the cultural food that we have drunk in from our mothers' breasts. The distinctively American spirit—pioneer, as distinguished from the reminiscently English—that appears in Whitman and Emerson and James, has had to exist on sufferance alongside of this other cult, unconsciously belittled by our cultural makers of opinion. No country has perhaps had so great indigenous genius which had so little influence on the country's traditions and expressions. The unpopular and dreaded German-American of the present day is a beginning amateur in comparison with those foolish Anglophiles of Boston and New York and Philadelphia whose reversion to cultural type sees uncritically in England's cause the cause of Civilization, and, under the guise of ethical independence of thought, carries along European traditions which are no more "American" than the German categories themselves.

It speaks well for German-American innocence of heart or else for its lack of imagination that it has not turned the hyphen stigma into a "Tu quoque!" If there were to be any hyphens scattered about, clearly they should be affixed to those English descendants who had had centuries of time to be made American where the German had had only half a century. Most significantly has the war brought out of them this alien virus, showing them still loving English things, owing allegiance to the English Kultur, moved by English shibboleths and prejudice. It is only because it has been the ruling class in this country that bestowed the epithets that we have not heard copiously and scornfully of "hyphenated English-Americans." But even our quarrels with England have had the bad temper, the extravagance, of family quarrels. The Englishman of to-day nags us and dislikes us in that personal, peculiarly intimate way in which he dislikes the Australian, or as we may dislike our younger brothers. He still thinks of us incorrigibly as "colonials." America—official, controlling, literary, political America—is still, as a writer recently expressed it, "culturally speaking, a self-governing dominion of the British Empire."

The non-English American can scarcely be blamed if he sometimes thinks of the Anglo-Saxon predominance in America as little more than a predominance of priority. The Anglo-Saxon was merely the first immigrant, the first to found a colony. He has never really ceased to be the descendant of immigrants, nor has he ever succeeded in transforming that colony into a real nation, with a tenacious, richly woven fabric of native culture. Colonials from the other nations have come and settled down beside him. They found no definite native culture which should startle them out of their colonialism, and consequently they looked back to their mother-country, as the earlier

Anglo-Saxon immigrant was looking back to his. What has been offered the newcomer has been the chance to learn English, to become a citizen, to salute the flag. And those elements of our ruling classes who are responsible for the public schools, the settlements, all the organizations for amelioration in the cities, have every reason to be proud of the care and labor which they have devoted to absorbing the immigrant. His opportunities the immigrant has taken to gladly, with almost a pathetic eagerness to make his way in the new land without friction or disturbance. The common language has made not only for the necessary communication, but for all the amenities of life.

If freedom means the right to do pretty much as one pleases, so long as one does not interfere with others, the immigrant has found freedom, and the ruling element has been singularly liberal in its treatment of the invading hordes. But if freedom means a democratic coöperation in determining the ideals and purposes and industrial and social institutions of a country, then the immigrant has not been free, and the Anglo-Saxon element is guilty of just what every dominant race is guilty of in every European country: the imposition of its own culture upon the minority peoples. The fact that this imposition has been so mild and, indeed, semi-conscious does not alter its quality. And the war has brought out just the degree to which that purpose of "Americanizing," that is to say, "Anglo-Saxonizing," the immigrant has failed.

For the Anglo-Saxon now in his bitterness to turn upon the other peoples, talk about their "arrogance," scold them for not being melted in a pot which never existed, is to betray the unconscious purpose which lay at the bottom of his heart. It betrays too the possession of a racial jealousy similar to that of which he is now accusing the so-called "hyphenates." Let the Anglo-Saxon be proud enough of the heroic toil and heroic sacrifices which moulded the nation. But let him ask himself, if he had had to depend on the English descendants, where he would have been living to-day. To those of us who see in the exploitation of unskilled labor the strident red *leit-motif* of our civilization, the settling of the country presents a great social drama as the waves of immigration broke over it.

Let the Anglo-Saxon ask himself where he would have been if these races had not come? Let those who feel the inferiority of the non-Anglo-Saxon immigrant contemplate that region of the States which has remained the most distinctively "American," the South. Let him ask himself whether he would really like to see the foreign hordes Americanized into such an Americanization. Let him ask himself how superior this native civilization is to the great "alien" states of Wisconsin and Minnesota, where Scandinavians, Poles, and Germans have self-consciously labored to preserve their traditional culture, while being outwardly and satisfactorily American. Let him ask himself how much more wisdom, intelligence, industry and social leadership has come out of these alien states than out of all the truly American ones. The South, in fact, while this vast Northern development has gone on, still remains an English colony, stagnant and complacent, having progressed culturally scarcely beyond the early Victorian era. It is culturally sterile because it has had no advantage of cross-fertilization like the Northern states. What has happened in states such as Wisconsin and Minnesota is that strong foreign cultures have struck root in a new and fertile soil. America has meant liberation, and German and Scandinavian political ideas and social energies have expanded to a new potency. The process has not been at all the fancied "assimilation" of the Scandinavian or Teuton. Rather has it been a process of their assimilation of us—I speak as an Anglo-Saxon. The foreign cultures have not been melted down or run together, made into some homogeneous Americanism, but have remained distinct but coöperating to the greater glory and benefit, not only of themselves but of all the native "Americanism" around them.

What we emphatically do not want is that these distinctive qualities should be washed out into a tasteless, colorless fluid of uniformity. Already we have far too much of this insipidity,—masses of people who are cultural half-breeds, neither assimilated Anglo-Saxons nor nationals of another culture. Each national colony in this country seems to retain in its foreign press, its vernacular literature, its schools, its intellectual and patriotic leaders, a central cultural nucleus. From this nucleus the colony extends out by imperceptible gradations to a fringe where national characteristics are all but lost. Our cities are filled with these half-breeds who retain their foreign names but have lost the foreign savor. This does not mean that they have actually been changed into New Englanders or Middle Westerners. It does not mean that they have been really Americanized. It means that, letting slip from them whatever native culture they had, they have substituted for it only the most rudimentary American—the American culture of the cheap newspaper, the "movies," the popular song, the ubiquitous automobile. The unthinking who survey this class call them assimilated, Americanized. The great American public school has done its work. With these people our institutions are safe. We may thrill with dread at the aggressive hyphenate, but this tame flabbiness is accepted as Americanization. The same moulders of opinion whose ideal is to melt the different races into Anglo-Saxon gold hail this poor product as the satisfying result of their alchemy.

Yet a truer cultural sense would have told us that it is not the self-conscious cultural nuclei that sap at our American life, but these fringes. It is not the Jew who sticks proudly to the faith of his fathers and boasts of that venerable culture of his who is dangerous to America, but the Jew who has lost the Jewish fire and become a mere elementary, grasping animal. It is not the Bohemian who supports the Bohemian schools in Chicago whose influence is sinister, but the Bohemian who has made money and has got into ward politics. Just so surely as we tend to disintegrate these nuclei of nationalistic culture do we tend to create hordes of men and women without a spiritual country, cultural outlaws, without taste, without standards but those of the mob. We sentence them to live on the most rudimentary planes of American life. The influences at the center of the nuclei are centripetal. They make for the intelligence and the social values which mean an enhancement of life. And just because the foreign-born retains this expressiveness is he likely to be a better citizen of the American community. The influences at the fringe, however, are centrifugal, anarchical. They make for detached fragments of peoples. Those who came to find liberty achieve only license. They become the flotsam and jetsam of American life, the downward undertow of our civilization with its leering cheapness and falseness of taste and spiritual outlook, the absence of mind and sincere feeling which we see in our slovenly towns, our vapid moving pictures, our popular novels, and in the vacuous faces of the crowds on the city street. This is the cultural wreckage of our time, and it is from the fringes of the Anglo-Saxon as well as the other stocks that it falls. America has as yet no impelling integrating force. It makes too easily for this detritus of cultures. In our loose, free country, no constraining national purpose, no tenacious folk-tradition and folk-style hold the people to a line.

The war has shown us that not in any magical formula will this purpose be found. No intense nationalism of the European plan can be ours. But do we not begin to see a new and more adventurous ideal? Do we not see how the national colonies in America, deriving power from the deep cultural heart of Europe and yet living here in mutual toleration, freed from the age-long tangles of races, creeds, and dynasties, may work out a federated ideal? America is transplated Europe, but a Europe that has not been disintegrated and scattered in the transplanting as in some Dispersion. Its colonies live here inextricably mingled, yet not homogeneous. They merge but they do not fuse.

America is a unique sociological fabric, and it bespeaks poverty of imagination not to be thrilled at the incalculable potentialities of so novel a union of men. To seek no other goal than the weary old nationalism,—belligerent, exclusive, inbreeding, the poison of which we are witnessing now in Europe,—is to make patriotism a hollow sham, and to declare that, in spite of our boastings, America must ever be a follower and not a leader of nations.

II

If we come to find this point of view plausible, we shall have to give up the search for our native "American" culture. With the exception of the South and that New England which, like the Red Indian, seems to be passing into solemn oblivion, there is no distinctively American culture. It is apparently our lot rather to be a federation of cultures. This we have been for half a century, and the war has made it ever more evident that this is what we are destined to remain. This will not mean, however, that there are not expressions of indigenous genius that could not have sprung from any other soil. Music, poetry, philosophy, have been singularly fertile and new. Strangely enough, American genius has flared forth just in those directions which are least understood of the people. If the American note is bigness, action, the objective as contrasted with the reflective life, where is the epic expression of this spirit? Our drama and our fiction, the peculiar fields for the expression of action and objectivity, are somehow exactly the fields of the spirit which remain poor and mediocre. American materialism is in some way inhibited from getting into impressive artistic form its own energy with which it bursts. Nor is it any better in architecture, the least romantic and subjective of all the arts. We are inarticulate of the very values which we profess to idealize. But in the finer forms—music, verse, the essay, philosophy—the American genius puts forth work equal to any of its contemporaries. Just in so far as our American genius has expressed the pioneer spirit, the adventurous, forward-looking drive of a colonial empire, is it representative of that whole America of the many races and peoples, and not of any partial or traditional enthusiasm. And only as that pioneer note is sounded can we really speak of the American culture. As long as we thought of Americanism in terms of the "melting-pot," our American cultural tradition lay in the past. It was something to which the new Americans were to be moulded. In the light of our changing ideal of Americanism, we must perpetrate the paradox that our American cultural tradition lies in the future. It will be what we all together make out of this incomparable opportunity of attacking the future with a new key.

Whatever American nationalism turns out to be, it is certain to become something utterly different from the nationalisms of twentieth-century Europe. This wave of reactionary enthusiasm to play the orthodox nationalistic game which is passing over the country is scarcely vital enough to last. We cannot swagger and thrill to the same national self-feeling. We must give new edges to our pride. We must be content to avoid the unnumbered woes that national patriotism has brought in Europe, and that fiercely heightened pride and self-consciousness. Alluring as this is, we must allow our imaginations to transcend this scarcely veiled belligerency. We can be serenely too proud to fight if our pride embraces the creative forces of civilization which armed contest nullifies. We can be too proud to fight if our code of honor transcends that of the schoolboy on the playground surrounded by his jeering mates. Our honor must be positive and creative, and not the mere jealous and negative protectiveness against metaphysical violations of our technical rights. When the doctrine is put forth that in one American flows the mystic blood of all our country's sacred honor, freedom, and prosperity, so that an injury to him is to be the signal for turning our whole nation into that clan-feud of horror and reprisal which would be war, then we find ourselves back among the musty schoolmen of the Middle Ages, and not in any pragmatic and realistic America of the twentieth century.

We should hold our gaze to what America has done, not what mediaeval codes of dueling she has failed to observe. We have transplanted European modernity to our soil, without the spirit that inflames it and turns all its energy into mutual destruction. Out of these foreign peoples there has somehow been squeezed the poison. An America, "hyphenated" to bitterness, is somehow non-explosive. For, even if we all hark back in sympathy to a European nation, even if the war has set every one vibrating to some emotional string twanged on the other side of the Atlantic, the effect has been one of almost dramatic harmlessness.

What we have really been witnessing, however unappreciatively, in this country has been a thrilling and bloodless battle of Kulturs. In that arena of friction which has been the most dramatic—between the hyphenated German-American and the hyphenated English-American—there have emerged rivalries of philosophies which show up deep traditional attitudes, points of view which accurately reflect the gigantic issues of the war. America has mirrored the spiritual issues. The vicarious struggle has been played out peacefully here in the mind. We have seen the stout resistiveness of the old moral interpretation of history on which Victorian England throve and made itself great in its own esteem. The clean and immensely satisfying vision of the war as a contest between right and wrong; the enthusiastic support of the Allies as the incarnation of virtue-on-a-rampage; the fierce envisaging of their selfish national purposes as the ideals of justice, free-

dom and democracy—all this has been thrown with intensest force against the German realistic interpretations in
terms of the struggle for power and the virility of the integrated State. America has been the intellectual battleground of the nations.

III

The failure of the melting-pot, far from closing the
great American democratic experiment, means that it has
only just begun. Whatever American nationalism turns
out to be, we see already that it will have a color richer
and more exciting than our ideal has hitherto encom-
passed. In a world which has dreamed of internationalism, we find that we have all unawares been building up
the first international nation. The voices which have cried
for a tight and jealous nationalism of the European pattern are failing. From that ideal, however valiantly and
disinterestedly it has been set for us, time and tendency
have moved us further and further away. What we have
achieved has been rather a cosmopolitan federation of national colonies, of foreign cultures, from which the sting
of devastating competition has been removed. America is
already the world-federation in miniature, the continent
where for the first time in history has been achieved that
miracle of hope, the peaceful living side by side, with
character substantially preserved, of the most heterogene-

ous peoples under the sun. Nowhere else has such contiguity been anything but the breeder of misery. Here, notwithstanding our tragic failures of adjustment, the outlines are already too clear not to give us a new vision and a new orientation of the American mind in the world.

It is for the American of the younger generation to accept this cosmopolitanism, and carry it along with self-conscious and fruitful purpose. In his colleges, he is already getting, with the study of modern history and politics, the modern literatures, economic geography, the privilege of a cosmopolitan outlook such as the people of no other nation of to-day in Europe can possibly secure. If he is still a colonial, he is no longer the colonial of one partial culture, but of many. He is a colonial of the world. Colonialism has grown into cosmopolitanism, and his motherhood is not one nation, but all who have anything life-enhancing to offer to the spirit. That vague sympathy which the France of ten years ago was feeling for the world—a sympathy which was drowned in the terrible reality of war—may be the modern American's, and that in a positive and aggressive sense. If the American is parochial, it is in sheer wantonness or cowardice. His provincialism is the measure of his fear of bogies or the defect of his imagination.

Indeed, it is not uncommon for the eager Anglo-Saxon who goes to a vivid American university to-day to find his true friends not among his own race but among the acclimatized German or Austrian, the acclimatized Jew, the acclimatized Scandinavian or Italian. In them he finds the cosmopolitan note. In these youths, foreign-born or the children of foreign-born parents, he is likely to find many of his old inbred morbid problems washed away. These friends are oblivious to the repressions of that tight little society in which he so provincially grew up. He has a pleasurable sense of liberation from the stale and familiar attitudes of those whose ingrowing culture has scarcely created anything vital for his American of to-day. He breathes a larger air. In his new enthusiasms for continental literature, for unplumbed Russian depths, for French clarity of thought, for Teuton philosophies of power, he feels himself citizen of a larger world. He may be absurdly superficial, his outward-reaching wonder may ignore all the stiller and homelier virtues of his Anglo-Saxon home, but he has at least found the clue to that international mind which will be essential to all men and women of goodwill if they are ever to save this Western world of ours from suicide. His new friends have gone through a similar evolution. America has burned most of the baser metal also from them. Meeting now with this common American background, all of them may yet retain that distinctiveness of their native cultures and their national spiritual slants. They are more valuable and interesting to each other for being different, yet that difference could not be creative were it not for this new cosmopolitan outlook which America has given them and which they all equally possess.

A college where such a spirit is possible even to the smallest degree, has within itself already the seeds of this international intellectual world of the future. It suggests that the contribution of America will be an intellectual internationalism which goes far beyond the mere exchange of scientific ideas and discoveries and the cold recording of facts. It will be an intellectual sympathy which is not satisfied until it has got at the heart of the different cultural expressions, and felt as they feel. It may have immense preferences, but it will make understanding and not indignation its end. Such a sympathy will unite and not divide.

Against the thinly disguised panic which calls itself "patriotism" and the thinly disguised militarism which calls itself "preparedness" the cosmopolitan ideal is set. This does not mean that those who hold it are for a policy of drift. They, too, long passionately for an integrated and disciplined America. But they do not want one which is integrated only for domestic economic exploitation of the workers or for predatory economic imperialism among the weaker peoples. They do not want one that is integrated by coercion or militarism, or for the truculent assertion of a mediaeval code of honor and of doubtful rights. They believe that the most effective integration will be one which coördinates the diverse elements and turns them consciously toward working out together the place of America in the world-situation. They demand for integration a genuine integrity, a wholeness and soundness of enthusiasm and purpose which can only come when no national colony within our America feels that it is being discriminated against or that its cultural case is being prejudged. This strength of coöperation, this feeling that all who are here may have a hand in the destiny of America, will make for a finer spirit of integration than any narrow "Americanism" or forced chauvinism.

In this effort we may have to accept some form of that dual citizenship which meets with so much articulate horror among us. Dual citizenship we may have to recognize as the rudimentary form of that international citizenship to which, if our words mean anything, we aspire. We have assumed unquestioningly that mere participation in the political life of the United States must cut the new citizen off from all sympathy with his old allegiance. Anything but a bodily transfer of devotion from one sovereignty to another has been viewed as a sort of moral treason against the Republic. We have insisted that the immigrant whom we welcomed escaping from the very exclusive nationalism of his European home shall forthwith adopt a nationalism just as exclusive, just as narrow, and even less legitimate because it is founded on no warm traditions of his own. Yet a nation like France is said to permit a formal and legal dual citizenship even at the present time. Though a citizen of hers may pretend to cast off his allegiance in favor of some other sovereignty, he is still subject to her laws when he returns. Once a citizen, always a citizen, no matter how many new citizenships he may embrace. And such a dual citizenship seems to us sound and right. For it recognizes that, although the Frenchman may accept the formal institutional framework of his new country and indeed become intensely loyal to it, yet his

Frenchness he will never lose. What makes up the fabric of his soul will always be of this Frenchness, so that unless he becomes utterly degenerate he will always to some degree dwell still in his native environment.

Indeed, does not the cultivated American who goes to Europe practise a dual citizenship, which, if not formal, is no less real? The American who lives abroad may be the least expatriate of men. If he falls in love with French ways and French thinking and French democracy and seeks to saturate himself with the new spirit, he is guilty of at least a dual spiritual citizenship. He may be still American, yet he feels himself through sympathy also a Frenchman. And he finds that this expansion involves no shameful conflict within him, no surrender of his native attitude. He has rather for the first time caught a glimpse of the cosmopolitan spirit. And after wandering about through many races and civilizations he may return to America to find them all here living vividly and crudely, seeking the same adjustment that he made. He sees the new peoples here with a new vision. They are no longer masses of aliens, waiting to be "assimilated," waiting to be melted down into the indistinguishable dough of Anglo-Saxonism. They are rather threads of living and potent cultures, blindly striving to weave themselves into a novel international nation, the first the world has seen. In an Austria-Hungary or a Prussia the stronger of these cultures would be moving almost instinctively to subjugate the weaker. But in America those wills-to-power are turned in a different direction into learning how to live together

Along with dual citizenship we shall have to accept, I think, that free and mobile passage of the immigrant between America and his native land again which now arouses so much prejudice among us. We shall have to accept the immigrant's return for the same reason that we consider justified our own flitting about the earth. To stigmatize the alien who works in America for a few years and returns to his own land, only perhaps to seek American fortune again, is to think in narrow nationalistic terms. It is to ignore the cosmopolitan significance of this migration. It is to ignore the fact that the returning immigrant is often a missionary to an inferior civilization.

This migratory habit has been especially common with the unskilled laborers who have been pouring into the United States in the last dozen years from every country in southeastern Europe. Many of them return to spend their earnings in their own country or to serve their country in war. But they return with an entirely new critical outlook, and a sense of the superiority of American organization to the primitive living around them. This continued passage to and fro has already raised the material standard of living in many regions of these backward countries. For these regions are thus endowed with exactly what they need, the capital for the exploitation of their natural resources, and the spirit of enterprise. America is thus educating these laggard peoples from the very bottom of society up, awaking vast masses to a new-born hope for the future. In the migratory Greek, therefore, we have not the parasitic alien, the doubtful American asset, but a symbol of that cosmopolitan interchange which is coming, in spite of all war and national exclusiveness.

Only America, by reason of the unique liberty of opportunity and traditional isolation for which she seems to stand, can lead in this cosmopolitan enterprise. Only the American—and in this category I include the migratory alien who has lived with us and caught the pioneer spirit and a sense of new social vistas—has the chance to become that citizen of the world. America is coming to be, not a nationality but a trans-nationality, a weaving back and forth, with the other lands, of many threads of all sizes and colors. Any movement which attempts to thwart this weaving, or to dye the fabric any one color, or disentangle the threads of the strands, is false to this cosmopolitan vision. I do not mean that we shall necessarily glut ourselves with the raw product of humanity. It would be folly to absorb the nations faster than we could weave them. We have no duty either to admit or reject. It is purely a question of expediency. What concerns us is the fact that the strands are here. We must have a policy and an ideal for an actual situation. Our question is, What shall we do with our America? How are we likely to get the more creative America—by confining our imaginations to the ideal of the melting-pot, or broadening them to some such cosmopolitan conception as I have been vaguely sketching?

We cannot Americanize America worthily by sentimentalizing and moralizing history. When the best schools are expressly renouncing the questionable duty of teaching patriotism by means of history, it is not the time to force shibboleth upon the immigrant. This form of Americanization has been heard because it appealed to the vestiges of our old sentimentalized and moralized patriotism. This has so far held the field as the expression of the new American's new devotion. The inflections of other voices have been drowned. They must be heard. We must see if the lesson of the war has not been for hundreds of these later Americans a vivid realization of their transnationality, a new consciousness of what America means to them as a citizenship in the world. It is the vague historic idealisms which have provided the fuel for the European flame. Our American ideal can make no progress until we do away with this romantic gilding of the past.

All our idealisms must be those of future social goals in which all can participate, the good life of personality lived in the environment of the Beloved Community. No mere doubtful triumphs of the past, which redound to the glory of only one of our trans-nationalities, can satisfy us. It must be a future America, on which all can unite, which pulls us irresistibly toward it, as we understand each other more warmly.

To make real this striving amid dangers and apathies is work for a younger intelligentsia of America. Here is an enterprise of integration into which we can all pour ourselves, of a spiritual welding which should make us, if the final menace ever came, not weaker, but infinitely strong.

A Mirror of The Middle West

NO EASTERNER, born forlornly within the sphere of New York, Boston, or Philadelphia, can pass very far beyond the Alleghanies without feeling that American civilization is here found in the full tide of believing in itself. The flat countryside looks more ordered, more farmlike; the Main Streets that flash by the car-windows somehow look more robust and communal. There may be no less litter and scrubbiness; the clustered houses of the towns may look even more flimsy, undistinguished, well-worn; but it is a litter of aspiring order, a chaos which the people are insensitive to because they are living in the light of a hopeful future. The East has pretty much abandoned itself to the tides of immigration and industrial change which have overwhelmed it: no one really believes that anything startling will be done to bring about a new heaven and a new earth. But the intelligence of the West seems to live in apocalyptic sociological—not socialistic, however—dreams. Architects and business men combine half-heartedly to "save New York" from the horrors of the Jewish clothing-trade invasion, but Chicago draws great maps and sketches of a city-planning that shall make it not only habitable but radiant and palatial.

Hope has not vanished from the East, but it has long since ceased to be our daily diet. Europe has infected us perhaps with some of its world-weariness. The East produces more skeptics and spiritual malcontents than the West. For the Middle West seems to have accomplished most of the things, industrial and political, that the East has been trying to do, and it has done them better. The Middle West is the apotheosis of American civilization, and like all successes it is in no mood to be very critical of itself or very examinatory as to the anatomy and physiology of its social being. No Easterner with Meredith Nicholson's human and literary experience would write so complacently and cheerfully about his part of the country as Mr. Nicholson writes about "The Valley of Democracy." His self-confidence is the very voice of the Middle West, telling us what it thinks of itself. This, we say as we read, must be the inner candor which goes with the West that we see with our eyes. So we like Mr. Nicholson's articles not so much for the information they give us as for the attitudes they let slip, the unconscious revelations of what the people he is talking for think important.

It is not a book of justification, although he would anxiously have us take not too seriously the political vagaries like Bryanism and Progressivism. And he wishes us to miss none of the symphony orchestras and art institutes that evidently now begin to grow like grasshoppers on the prairies. He treats himself rather as an expositor, and he is explicitly informational, almost as if for a foreign country. He sometimes has an amusing air of having hastily read up and investigated Western wonders and significances that have been not only common material in the Eastern magazines, but matter of despairing admiration on the part of those of us who are general improvers of mankind. He is naïve about the greatness of Chicago, the vastness of agricultural production, the ravages of culture among the middle classes. He is almost the professional Westerner showing off his prize human stock.

Mr. Nicholson does well to begin with the folksiness of the West. No one who has experienced that fine open friendliness of the prosperous Middle Westerner, that pleasant awareness of the alert and beneficent world we live in, can deny that the Middle West is quite justified in thinking of itself as the real heart of the nation. That belief in the ultimate good sense, breadth of vision, and devotion to the common good, of the "folks back home," is in itself a guaranty of social stability and of a prosperity which implies that things will never be any different except as they slowly improve. Who can say that we have no Gemütlichkeit in America, when he runs up against this warm social mixability which goes so far to compensate for the lack of intellectual *nuances* and spontaneous artistic sensibilities?

Of course the Middle West has to pay for its social responsiveness in a failure to create, at least in this day and generation, very vigorous and diverse spiritual types. An excessive amiability, a genius for adaptability will, in the end, put a premium on conformity. The Westerner sincerely believes that he is more averse to conventionality than the Easterner, but the latter does not find him so. The heretic seems to have a much harder time of it in the West. Classes and attitudes that have offended against the "folks' " codes may be actually outlawed. When there are acute differences of opinion, as in the war, society splits into bitter and irreconcilable camps, whereas in the East the undesirables have been allowed to shade off towards limbo in gradual degrees. When hatred and malice, too long starved by too much "niceness," do break out from the natural man, they may produce those waves of persecution and vindictiveness which, coming from a so recently pacifist West, astonished an East that was no less densely saturated with aliens but was more conversant with the feeling that it takes all kinds of people to make a world. Folksiness evidently has its dark underlining in a tendency to be stampeded by herd-emotion. "Social conscience" may become the duty to follow what the mob demands, and democracy may come to mean that the individual feels himself somehow expressed—his private tastes and intelligence—in whatever the crowd chooses to do.

I have followed Mr. Nicholson in his speaking of the Middle West as if he thought of the region as a unit. He does speak as if he did, but he does not really mean it. Much as he would like to believe in the substantial equality of the people in the Valley of Democracy, he cannot help letting us see that it is but one class that he has in mind—his own, the prosperous people of the towns. He protests against their being scornfully waved aside as bourgeoisie. "They constitute the most interesting and admirable of our social strata." And he is quite right. Certainly this stratum is by far the most admirable of all the middle classes of the world. It is true that "nowhere else have comfort, opportunity, and aspiration produced the same combination." He marvels at the numbers of homes in the cities that cannot imaginably be supported on less than five thousand a year. And it is these homes, and their slightly more impoverished neighbors, who are for him the "folks," the incarnate Middle West. The proletarian does not exist for him. The working-classes are merely so much cement, filling in the bricks of the temple—or, better, folks in embryo, potential owners of bungalows on pleasant suburban streets. Mr. Nicholson's enthusiasm is for the college-girl wife, who raises babies, attends women's clubs, and is not afraid to dispense with the unattainable servant. It is for the good-natured and public-spirited business man, who goes into politics because politics in the Middle West has always been concerned with the prosperity of the business community. But about the economic foundation of this class Mr. Nicholson sounds as innocent as a babe.

Take his attitude towards the farmer. You gather from these pages that in the Middle West the farmer is a somewhat unfortunate anomaly, a shadow on the bright scene. Farming is scarcely even a respectable profession: "the great-grandchildren of the Middle Western pioneers are not easily persuaded that farming is an honorable calling"! He hints darkly at a decay in fiber. Only one chapter out of six is given to the farmer, and that is largely occupied with the exertions of state agencies, universities, to lift him out of his ignorance and selfishness. The average farmer has few of the admirable qualities of the Valley of Democracy. He is not "folksy"; he is suspicious, conservative, somewhat embittered, little given to coöperation; he even needed prodding with his Liberty bonds. In Mr. Nicholson's pages the farmer becomes a huge problem which lies on the brain and conscience of a Middle West that can only act towards him in its best moments like a sort of benevolent Charity Organization Society. "To the average urban citizen," says Mr. Nicholson, "farming is something remote and uninteresting, carried on by men he never meets in regions that he only observes hastily from a speeding automobile or the window of a limited train."

It would take whole volumes to develop the implications of that sentence. Remember that that urban citizen is Mr. Nicholson's Middle West, and that the farmer comprises the huge bulk of the population. Is this not interesting, the attitude of the prosperous minority of an urban minority—a small but significant class which has in its hands all the non-productive business and political power —towards the great productive mass of the people? Could class division be revealed in plainer terms? This Middle West of Mr. Nicholson's class sees itself as not only innocent of exploitation, but full of all the personal and social virtues besides. But does the farmer see this class in this light? He does not. And Mr. Veblen has given us in one of his books an analysis of this society which may explain why: "The American country town and small city," he says, "is a business community, that is to say it lives for and by business traffic, primarily of a merchandising sort. ... Municipal politics is conducted as in some sort a public or overt extension of that private or covert organization of local interests that watches over the joint pecuniary benefit of the local businessmen. It is a means ... of safe-guarding the local business community against interlopers and against any evasive tactics on the part of the country population that serves as a host. ... The country town is a product and exponent of the American land system. In its beginning it is located and 'developed' as an enterprise of speculation in land values; that is to say, it is a business-like endeavor to get something for nothing by engrossing as much as may be of the increment of land values due to the increase of population and the settlement and cultivation of the adjacent agricultural area. It never (hitherto) loses this character of real-estate speculation. This affords a common bond and a common ground of pecuniary interest, which commonly masquerades under the name of public patriotism, public spirit, civic pride, and the like."

In other words, Town, in the traditional American scheme of things, is shown charging Country all the traffic will bear. It would be hard to find a member of Mr. Nicholson's Middle West—that minority urban class—who was not owing his prosperity to some form of industrial or real-estate speculation, of brokerage business enterprise, or landlordism. This class likes to say sometimes that it is "carrying the farmer." It would be more like the truth to say that the farmer is carrying this class. Country ultimately has to support Town; and Town, by holding control of the channels of credit and market, can make the farmer pay up to the hilt for the privilege of selling it his product. And does. When the farmers, getting a sense of the true workings of the society they live in, combine in a Non-Partisan League to control the organism of market and credit, they find they have a bitter class war on their hands. And the authentic voice of Mr. Nicholson here scolds them roundly for their restlessness and sedition. In this ferocious reaction of Town against Country's socialistic efforts to give itself economic autonomy, we get the betrayal of the social malaise of the Middle West, a confession of the cleavage of latent class conflict in a society as exploitative, as steeply tilted, as tragically extreme in its poles of well-being, as any other modern society based on the economic absolutism of property.

A large part of the hopefulness, the spiritual comfort of the Middle West, of its sturdy belief in itself, must be based on the inflexible reluctance of its intelligentsia to any such set of ideas. However thoroughly Marxian ideas may have saturated the thought of Europe and become the intellectual explosive of social change, the Middle West, as in this book, persists in its robust resistance to any such analysis or self-knowledge. It is not that Mr. Nicholson's attitudes are not true. It is that they are so very much less than the whole truth. They need to be supplemented by analysis set in the terms in which the progressive minds of the rest of the world are thinking. The intelligent Middle West needs to sacrifice a certain amount of complacency in exchange for an understanding of the structure of its own society. It would then realize that to read "The Valley of Democracy" in conjunction with pages 315-323 of Veblen's "Imperial Germany and the Industrial Revolution" is to experience one of the most piquant intellectual adventures granted to the current mind.

This Older Generation

I

I READ with ever-increasing wonder the guarded defenses and discreet apologies for the older generation which keep filtering through the essays of the *Atlantic*. I can even seem to detect a growing decision of tone, a definite assurance of conviction, which seems to imply that a rally has been undertaken against the accusations which the younger generation, in its self-assurance, its irreverence for the old conventions and moralities, its passion for the novel and startling, seemed to be bringing against them. The first faint twinges of conscience felt by the older generation have given place to renewed homily. There is an evident anxiety to get itself put on record as perfectly satisfied with its world, and desirous that its sons and daughters should learn anew of those peculiar beauties in which it has lived. Swept off its feet by the call to social service and social reform, it is slowly regaining its foundation, and, slightly flushed, and with garments somewhat awry, it proclaims again its belief in the eternal verities of Protestant religion and conventional New England morality.

It is always an encouraging sign when people are rendered self-conscious and are forced to examine the basis of their ideals. The demand that they explain them to skeptics always makes for clarity. When the older generation is put on the defensive, it must first discover what convictions it has, and then sharpen them to their finest point in order to present them convincingly. There are always too many unquestioned things in the world, and for a person or class to have to scurry about to find reasons for its prejudices is about as healthy an exercise as one could wish for either of them. To be sure, the reasons are rarely any more than *ex post facto* excuses,—supports and justifications for the prejudices rather than the causes thereof. Reason itself is very seldom more than that. The important point is that one should feel the need of a reason. This always indicates that something has begun to slide, that the world is no longer so secure as it was, that obvious truths no longer are obvious, that the world has begun to bristle with question marks.

One of the basic grievances of this older generation against the younger of to-day, with its social agitation, its religious heresy, its presumptive individuality, its economic restlessness, is that all this makes it uncomfortable. When you have found growing older to be a process of the reconciliation of the spirit to life, it is decidedly disconcerting to have some youngster come along and point out the irreconcilable things in the universe. Just as you have made a tacit agreement to call certain things non-existent, it is highly discommoding to have somebody shout with strident tones that they are very real and significant. When, after much struggling and compromise, you have got your world clamped down, it is discouraging to have a gale arise which threatens to blow over all your structure. Through so much of the current writing runs this quiet note of disapprobation. These agnostic professors who unsettle the faith of our youth, these "intellectuals who stick a finger in everybody's pie in the name of social justice," these sensation-mongers who unveil great masses of political and social corruption, these remorseless scientists who would reveal so many of our reticences—why can't they let us alone? Can they not see that God's in his heaven, all's right with the world?

II

Now I know this older generation which doth protest so much. I have lived with it for the last fifteen years, ever since I began to wonder whether all was for the best in the best of all possible worlds. I was educated by it, grew up with it. I doubt if any generation ever had a more docile pupil than I. What they taught me, I find they still believe, or at least so many of them as have not gone over to the enemy, or been captured by the militant youth of to-day. Or, as seems rather likely, they no longer precisely believe, but they want their own arguments to convince themselves. It is probable that when we really believe a thing with all our hearts, we do not attempt to justify it. Justification comes only when we are beginning to doubt it.

By this older generation I mean, of course, the mothers and fathers and uncles and aunts of the youth of both sexes between twenty and thirty who are beginning their professional or business life. And I refer of course to the comfortable or fairly comfortable American middle class. Now this older generation has had a religion, a metaphysics, an ethics, and a political and social philosophy, which have reigned practically undisputed until the appearance of the present generation. It has at least never felt called upon to justify itself. It has never been directly challenged, as it is to-day. In order to localize this generation still further, we must see it in its typical setting of the small town or city, clustered about the institutions of church and family. If we have any society which can be called "American," it is this society. Its psychology is American psychology; its soul is America's soul.

This older generation, which I have known so well for fifteen years, has a religion which is on the whole as pleasant and easy as could be devised. Though its members are the descendants of the stern and rugged old Puritans, who wrestled with the devil and stripped their world of all that might seduce them from the awful service of God, they have succeeded in straining away by a long process all the repellent attitudes in the old philosophy of life. It is

297

unfair to say that the older generation believe in dogmas and creeds. It would be more accurate to say that it does not disbelieve. It retains them as a sort of guaranty of the stability of the faith, but leaves them rather severely alone. It does not even make more than feeble efforts to reinterpret them in the light of modern knowledge. They are useless, but necessary.

The foundation of this religion may be religious, but the superstructure is almost entirely ethical. Most sermons of to-day are little more than pious exhortations to good conduct. By good conduct is meant that sort of action which will least disturb the normal routine of modern middle-class life: common honesty in business life, faithfulness to duty, ambition in business and profession, filial obligation, the use of talents, and always and everywhere simple human kindness and love. The old Puritan ethics, which saw in the least issue of conduct a struggle between God and the devil, has become a mere code for facilitating the daily friction of conventional life.

Now one would indeed be churlish to find fault with this devout belief in simple goodness, which characterizes the older generation. It is only when these humble virtues are raised up into an all-inclusive program for social reform and into a philosophy of life, that one begins to question, and to feel afar the deep hostility of the older generation to the new faith.

Simple kindness, common honesty, filial obedience, it is evidently still felt, will solve all the difficulties of personal and social life. The most popular novels of the day are those in which the characters do the most good to each other. The enormous success with the older generation of *The Inside of the Cup, Queed,* and *V. V.'s Eyes,* is based primarily on the fact that these books represent a sublimated form of the good old American melodramatic moral sense. And now comes along Mr. Gerald Stanley Lee with his *Crowds,*—what a funny, individualized, personal-responsibility crowd he gives us, to be sure,—and his panacea for modern social ills by the old solution of applied personal virtue. Never a word about removing the barriers of caste and race and economic inequality, but only an urging to step over them. Never a trumpet-call to level the ramparts of privilege, or build up the heights of opportunity, but only an appeal to extend the charitable hand from the ramparts of heaven, or offer the kindly patronage to the less fortunate, or—most dazzling of all— throw away, in a frenzy of abandonment, life and fortune. Not to construct a business organization where dishonesty would be meaningless, but to be utopianly honest against the business world. In other words, the older generation believes in getting all the luxury of the virtue of goodness, while conserving all the advantages of being in a vicious society.

If there is any one characteristic which distinguishes the older generation, it is this belief that social ills may be cured by personal virtue. Its highest moral ideals are sacrifice and service. But the older generation can never see how intensely selfish these ideals are, in the most complete sense of the word selfish. What they mean always is, "I

sacrifice myself for you," "I serve you," not, "We coöperate in working ceaselessly toward an ideal where all may
be free and none may be served or serve." These ideals of
sacrifice and service are utterly selfish, because they take
account only of the satisfaction and moral consolidation of
the doer. They enhance his moral value; but what of the
person who is served or sacrificed for? What of the person
who is done good to? If the feelings of sacrifice and service
were in any sense altruistic, the moral enhancement of the
receiver would be the object sought. But can it not be said
that for every individual virtuous merit secured by an act
of sacrifice or service on the part of the doer, there is a
corresponding depression on the part of the receiver? Do
we not universally recognize this by calling a person who
is not conscious of this depression, a parasite, and the
person who is no longer capable of depression, a pauper?
It is exactly those free gifts, such as schools, libraries, and
so forth, which are impersonal or social, that we can accept
gratefully and gladly; and it is exactly because the minis-
trations of a Charity Organization Society are impersonal
and businesslike that they can be received willingly and
without moral depression by the poor.

The ideal of duty is equally open to attack. The great
complaint of the younger against the older generation has
to do with the rigidity of the social relationships into
which the younger find themselves born. The world seems
to be full of what may be called canalized emotions. One
is "supposed" to love one's aunt or one's grandfather in a
certain definite way, at the risk of being "unnatural." One

gets almost a sense of the quantitative measurement of emotion. Perhaps the greatest tragedy of family life is the useless energy that is expended by the dutiful in keeping these artificial channels open, and the correct amount of current running. It is exactly this that produces most infallibly the rebellion of the younger generation. To hear that one ought to love this or that person; or to hear loyalty spoken of, as the older generation so often speaks of it, as if it consisted in an allegiance to something which one no longer believes in,—this is what soonest liberates those forces of madness and revolt which bewilder spiritual teachers and guides. It is those dry channels of duty and obligation through which no living waters of emotion flow that it is the ideal of the younger generation to break up. They will have no network of emotional canals which are not brimming, no duties which are not equally loves.

But when they are loves, you have duty no longer meaning very much. Duty, like sacrifice and service, always implies a personal relation of individuals. You are always doing your duty to somebody or something. Always the taint of inequality comes in. You are morally superior to the person who has duty done to him. If that duty is not filled with good-will and desire, it is morally hateful, or at very best, a necessary evil,—one of those compromises with the world which must be made in order to get through it at all. But duty without good-will is a compromise with our present state of inequality, and to raise duty to the level of a virtue is to consecrate that state of inequality forevermore.

It is the same thing with service. The older generation has attempted an insidious compromise with the new social democracy by combining the words "social" and service." Under cover of the ideal of service it tries to appropriate to itself the glory of social work, and succeeds in almost convincing itself and the world that its Christianity has always held the same ideal. The faithful are urged to extend their activities. The assumption is that, by doing good to more individuals, you are thereby becoming social. But to speak of "social democracy," which of course means a freely coöperating, freely reciprocating society of equals, and "service," together, is a contradiction of terms. For, when you serve people or do good to them, you thereby render yourself unequal with them. You insult the democratic ideal. If the service is compulsory, it is menial and you are inferior. If voluntary, you are superior. The difference, however, is only academic. The entire Christian scheme is a clever but unsuccessful attempt to cure the evils of inequality by transposing the values. The slave serves gladly instead of servilely. That is, he turns his master into a slave. That is why good Christian people can never get over the idea that Socialism means simply the triumph of one class over another. Today the proletarian is down, the capitalist up. To-morrow the proletarian will be up and the capitalist down. To pull down the mighty from their seats and exalt them of low degree is the highest pitch to which Christian ethics ever attained. The failure of the older generation to recognize a higher ethic, the ethic of democracy, is the cause of all the trouble.

The notorious Victorian era, which in its secret heart this older generation still admires so much, accentuated all the latent individualism of Christian ethics, and produced a code which, without the rebellion of the younger generation, would have spiritually guaranteed forever all moral caste divisions and inequalities of modern society. The Protestant Church, in which this exaggerated ethic was enshrined, is now paying heavily the price of this debauch of ethical power. Its rapidly declining numbers show that human nature has an invincible objection to being individually saved. The Catholic Church, which saves men as members of the Beloved Community, and not as individuals, flourishes. When one is saved by Catholicism, one becomes a democrat, and not a spiritual snob and aristocrat, as one does through Calvinism. The older generation can never understand that superb loyalty which is loyalty to a community,—a loyalty which, paradoxical as it may seem, nourishes the true social personality in proportion as the individual sense is lessened. The Protestant Church in its tenacious devotion to the personal ideal of a Divine Master—the highest and most popular Christian ideal of to-day—shows how very far it still is away from the ideals and ethics of a social democracy, a life lived in the Beloved Community.

The sense of self-respect is the very keystone of the personality in whose defence all this individualistic philosophy has been carefully built up. The Christian virtues date from ages when there was a vastly greater number of morally depressed people than there is now. The tenacious survival of these virtues can be due only to the fact that they were valuable to the moral prestige of some class. Our older generation, with its emphasis on duty, sacrifice, and service, shows us very clearly what those interests were. I deliberately accuse the older generation of conserving and greatly strengthening these ideals, as a defensive measure. Morals are always the product of a situation; they reflect a certain organization of human relations which some class or group wishes to preserve. A moral code or set of ideals is always the invisible spiritual sign of a visible social grace. In an effort to retain the *status quo* of that world of inequalities and conventions in which they most comfortably and prosperously live, the older generation has stamped, through all its agencies of family, church and school, upon the younger generation, just those seductive ideals which would preserve its position. These old virtues upon which, however, the younger generation is already making guerilla warfare are simply the moral support with which the older generation buttresses its social situation.

The natural barriers and prejudices by which our elders are cut off from a freely flowing democracy are thus given a spiritual justification, and there is added for our elders the almost sensual luxury of leaping, by free grace, the barriers and giving themselves away. But the price has to be paid. Just as profits, in the socialist philosophy, are taken to be an abstraction from wages, through the economic power which one class has over another, so the virtues of the older generation may be said to be an abstraction from the virtue of other classes less favorably situated from a moral or personal point of view. Their swollen self-respect is at the expense of others.

How well we know the type of man in the older generation who has been doing good all his life! How his personality has thrived on it! How he has ceaselessly been storing away moral fat in every cranny of his soul! His goodness has been meat to him. The need and depression of other people has been, all unconsciously to him, the air which he has breathed. Without their compensating misfortune or sin, his goodness would have wilted and died. If good people would earnestly set to work to make the world uniformly healthy, courageous, beautiful, and prosperous, the field of their vocation would be constantly limited, and finally destroyed. That they so stoutly resist all philosophies and movements which have these ends primarily in view is convincing evidence of the fierce and jealous egoism which animates their so plausibly altruistic spirit. One suspects that the older generation does not want its vocation destroyed. It takes an heroic type of goodness to undermine all the foundations on which our virtue rests.

If then I object to the ethical philosophy of the older generation on the ground that it is too individualistic, and, under the pretense of altruism, too egoistic, I object to its general intellectuality as not individual enough. Intellectually the older generation seems to me to lead far too vegetative a life. It may be that this life has been lived on the heights, that these souls have passed through fires and glories, but there is generally too little objective evidence of this subjective fact. If the intuition which accompanies experience has verified all the data regarding God, the soul, the family, and so forth,—to quote one of the staunch- est defenders of the generation,—this verification seems to have been obtained rather that the issues might be promptly disposed of and forgotten. Certainly the older generation is rarely interested in the profounder issues of life. It never speaks of death,—the suggestion makes it uncomfortable. It shies in panic at hints of sex-issues. It seems resolute to keep life on as objective a plane as pos- sible. It is no longer curious about the motives and feel- ings of people. It seems singularly to lack the psychologi- cal sense. If it gossips, it recounts actions, effects; it rarely seeks to interpret. It tends more and more to treat human beings as moving masses of matter instead of as personali- ties filled with potent influence, or as absorbingly inter- esting social types, as I am sure the younger generation does.

The older generation seems no longer to generalize, al- though it gives every evidence of having once prodigiously generalized, for its world is all hardened and definite. There are the good and the criminal, and the poor, the people who can be called nice, and the ordinary people. The world is already plotted out. Now I am sure that the generalizations of the truly philosophical mind are very fluid and ephemeral. They are no sooner made than the mind sees their insufficiency and has to break them up. A new cutting is made, only in turn to be shaken and rearranged. This keeps the philosopher thinking all the time, and it makes his world a very uncertain place. But he at least runs no risk of hardening, and he has his eyes open to most experience.

I am often impressed with the fact that the older generation has grown weary of thinking. It has simply put up the bars in its intellectual shop-windows and gone off home to rest. It may well be that this is because it has felt so much sorrow that it does not want to talk about sorrow, or so much love that to interpret love tires it, or repulsed so many rude blows of destiny that it has no interest in speaking of destiny. Its flame may be low for the very reason that it has burned so intensely. But how many of the younger generation would eagerly long for such interpretations if the older would only reveal them! And how little plausible is that experience when it is occasionally interpreted! No, enthusiasm, passion for ideas, sensuality, religious fervor,—all the heated weapons with which the younger generation attacks the world, seem only to make the older generation uneasy. The spirit, in becoming reconciled to life, has lost life itself.

As I see the older generation going through its daily round of business, church, and family life, I cannot help feeling that its influence is profoundly pernicious. It has signally failed to broaden its institutions for the larger horizon of the time. The church remains a private club of comfortable middle-class families, while outside there grows up without spiritual inspiration a heterogeneous mass of people without ties, roots, or principles. The town changes from a village to an industrial center, and church and school go through their time-honored and listless motions. The world widens, society expands, formidable crises appear, but the older generation does not broaden, or if it does, the broadening is in no adequate proportion to our needs. The older generation still uses the old ideas for the new problem. Whatever new wine it finds must be poured into the old bottles.

Where are the leaders among the older generation in America who, with luminous faith and intelligence, are rallying around them the disintegrated numbers of idealistic youth, as Bergson and Barrès and Jaurès have done in France? A few years ago there seemed to be a promise of a forward movement toward Democracy, led by embattled veterans in a war against privilege. But how soon the older generation became wearied in the march! What is left now of that shining army and its leader? Must the younger generation eternally wait for the sign?

The answer is, of course, that it will not wait. It must shoulder the gigantic task of putting into practice its ideals and revolutionary points of view as wholeheartedly and successfully as our great-grandfathers applied theirs and tightened the philosophy of life which imprisons the older generation. The shuddering fear that we in turn may become weary, complacent, evasive, should be the best preventive of that stagnation. We shall never have done looking for the miracle, that it shall be given us to lighten, cheer, and purify our "younger generation," even as our older has depressed and disintegrated us.